I0479275

Sustainability in Fine Art:

A Gramscian Interpretation

Why ecological art can't save us

1

Victoria Slattery

An imprint of Boom Publications Ltd

272 Bath Street
Glasgow SCOTLAND
G2 4JR

Boom Graduates and the logo are trademarks of Boom Publications Ltd.

Boom Publications Ltd is a more-than-profit company, dedicating over half our profits to university scholarships for underprivileged students worldwide. In order to offset our carbon footprint, we also pledge to plant a tree for each graduation book commissioned.

Sustainability in Fine Art: A Gramscian Interpretation (why ecological art can't save us) was first published in Great Britain in 2023.

Typeset by Helen at Boom Graduates.
Printed and bound in the UK.

To find out more about our authors and books visit www.boomgraduates.com and sign up for our newsletters.

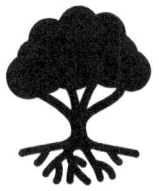

We plant a tree for every
Boom Graduate book commissioned, and
thereafter plant a tree for every 10 books sold.

Watch our forest grow at
https://moretrees.eco/forest/BoomPublicationsLtd/

Victoria Slattery

Sustainability in Fine Art: a Gramscian Interpretation
(*why ecological art can't save us*)

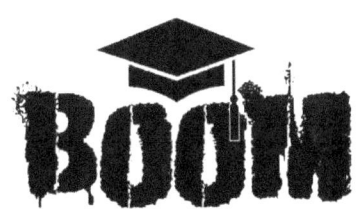

Victoria Slattery

Contents

Victoria Slattery

Abstract

T his study investigates the sustainability of the Fine Arts through the lens of Gramscian thinking. The theory of cultural hegemony is applied to the art world to understand how the arts are practiced in terms of sustainability. Additionally, ecological art is explored as a proponent of sustainability within the arts and in wider society. This study utilised a qualitative method to gather and analyse data, semi-structured interviews were carried out and analysed through thematic analysis to reveal relevant themes and concepts. Analysis and discussion determined that cultural hegemony is an appropriate theory to apply to the art world and can explain why the fine arts are unsustainable, they are operating within the wider economic system of capitalism and therefore share its production and consumption patterns. Encouraging excessive use of raw materials and carbon intensive techniques as well as sharing capitalisms class divide. The conflation of these factors is generating unsustainable practice in the arts.

Chapter One:

Introduction

Background

Antonio Gramsci was an Italian communist who engaged in political writings during his incarceration by Italy's fascist regime in 1926, ending only as the result of his death in 1937 (Rosengarten 1986). In Gramsci's resistance to the fascist regime, he explored why workers had not behaved the way Marx had predicted as a response to the constraints of advanced capitalism (Lears 1985). Marx predicted a working-class revolt against the capitalist regime, but this never came to pass (Marx

1996). Gramsci suggested that the workers did not revolt due to their existence within a cultural hegemony (Bates 1975). No specific definition of cultural hegemony exists within Gramsci's writings, however this study defines cultural hegemony as 'the spontaneous consent given by the great masses of the population to the general direction imposed on social life by the dominant fundamental group; this consent is historically caused by the prestige (and consequent confidence) which the dominant group enjoys because of its position and function in the world of production" (Lears 1985 p. 568).

Capitalist processes are deeply embedded into how the art world operates (Brown 2019), artworks are produced by artists for consumption by buyers and audiences. The production of the works, alongside their transportation and exhibition is a carbon intensive process that has consequences for ecological health. Giving rise to an unsustainable culture within the arts. Additionally, social forces contribute to the unsustainability prevailing within the arts, the class divide which subsists under capitalism is extrapolated to the class relations playing out within the art world (Howarth 2015; Fresia 2019). This maintains unsustainable behaviour as the working classes within the arts, defined in this study as artists occupying the lowest levels of the art market (Fresia 2019); engage in overproduction of their works to ascend to artistic and economic success which is accompanied by the excess use of raw materials and carbon intensive methods (Throsby 1994).

Ecological art is an opposing force regarding the unsustainability demonstrated within the art world; it is defined by this study as artworks that take in hand themes of activism and restoration, they draw their audience's attention to the interdependence of earth systems (Kagan et al 2014; Thornes 2008). The capability of ecological art to encourage a shift to more sustainable practice within the arts and to bring awareness and behaviour change to their audiences regarding sustainability is discussed within this paper (Thornes 2008). The viability of ecological art as a proponent of sustainable practice is limited as a result of the cultural hegemony. This is because the beliefs and values of the ruling class are in contrast with the aims of ecological art, therefore this study is investigating if ecological art can have any influence within the cultural hegemony of the arts.

Research questions

The following paper will aim to answer the four research questions stated below.

Q1. To what extent can Gramsci's theory of cultural hegemony be extrapolated to the Fine arts?

Q2. In terms of the effects of production and consumption of art works, how environmentally sustainable are the Fine arts?

Q3. How far does Gramsci's theory of cultural hegemony explain sustainability within Fine art?

Q4. How far can ecological art account for a shift towards sustainable behaviour within the arts and in wider society?

The subsequent research paper consists of a review of relevant literature, exploring the main theories and concepts to provide a rich background to the sustainability of the arts and why cultural hegemony is being utilised as the prevailing theoretical framework within this study. The following chapter will outline and evaluate the methodology used in this study to gather and analyse data in order to formulate conclusions to answer the research questions above. The next chapter will contain the findings of this research, as well as a discussion regarding these findings, discussion will link concepts and themes that emerged in chapter two to the findings of this study and being to formulate answers to the research questions. Finally, in chapter five conclusions will be drawn from the findings to answer the research questions and recommendations for further study will be outlined.

Chapter Two:

Literature Review

This literature review summarises the key schools of thought regarding the sustainability of the Fine Arts, reviews how immersed the industry is in the global economic system of capitalism and how this arguably creates a culture of unsustainability in several dimensions.

The boundaries between fine, applied arts and design have been blurred since the beginning of the English Arts and Crafts Movement (ACM) which took hold at the end of the 19th century (1880-1920) (V&A 2022). Prior to this movement there was a distinct separation between the two

17

branches of the arts, whereby the applied arts extrapolated exclusively to functional art, which in turn refers to aesthetic objects that serve a utilitarian purpose (Winter 1975). The English Arts and Crafts Movement represents a period when the production of art made a transfer from mass production to craftsmanship (Graf 2022). the ACM was closely linked with politics, as many important figures within the movement were part of the early socialist movement in Britain (Crawford 1997). Accordingly, a growing concern for environmental degradation and the social costs of the capitalist division of labour were prevailing among this demographic. This provided a catalyst for artists to create with a sense of socio-environmental stewardship (Winter 1975). Therefore, hand-made goods, produced by a skilled individual or craftsman were seen as more desirable (V&A 2022); promoting the individualism of the craftsman, as well as influencing smaller commercial firms, producing under the values of the ACM (Krugh 2014).

At the turn of the 20th century the ACM took its place as the dominant art movement in Britain (Crawford 1997). Additionally, taking hold overseas particularly in Germany, the US and for a moment in Japan during the Mingei movement (Chatterjee 2020). Despite its prevalence at the beginning of the century, after the First World War the ACM and its sentiments declined (Oliver 2004). The ACM foreshadowed the 'Modern Movement' as an established force within the arts (Amery 2009), as ACM's anti-machine stance lost credibility in a culture where mass production under liberal capitalism was already the dominant school of thought (Kaplan 2004). Additionally, the ACM relied significantly on bourgeoise capital. Flagship firms within the movement primarily furnished the homes of affluent industrialists (Kaplan 2004). This was due to the way these commodities were produced was cost intensive as a result of the personal method of making, thus only the rich could afford to purchase them (Crawford 1997). Consequently, the movement became the antithesis of itself due to the constraints of operating within industrial capitalism (Kaplan 2004).

The English Arts and Crafts Movement highlights that the effects of artistic production was and remains important to the art world. However, as the next section will outline, the production and consumption of art remains so deeply embedded within capitalism that despite the art world's concern for the negative impacts of production, true socio-environmental sustainability may be out of reach. At least for the foreseeable future, unless there are significant changes within the culture.

Q: Why is the Art World unsustainable?

A: Capitalism.

The art world is and always has been inherently economic (Throsby 1994). Artworks acquired based on their aesthetic appeal or as a financial asset can be resold, their price can rise over time, and they can represent a source of wealth or a source of speculative gain (Throsby 1994). This is because art works are highly regarded for their instrumental value, or how much they can be sold for rather, than value intrinsic to their existence (Caust 2007). Consequently, the artworld is deeply embedded into the global system of capitalism, and as a result falls victim to mass production, mass consumption and the ecological and social degradation that accompanies this (Throsby 1994).

The art world is not classically capitalist, as art is not (normally) mass produced and consumed in the same way most fashion, domestic goods or for instance cars would be (Hu 2013; Benjamin 1969). One piece of art is not produced uniformly hundreds or thousands of times and then sold to consumers – other than as second-hand reproductions. Mass production within the fine arts originated in the Renaissance period where artists were commissioned by their rich clients to create more and more art (Pritchard 2018). Art was (and remains) a commodity wealthy clients could obtain and showcase, reinforcing a culture of wealth and power; despite the high value ascribed to these works, artists were not necessarily paid fairly for their labour and struggled to make a living whilst the rich exploited their skills (Pritchard 2018). Hence, we start to see a division of labour emerging within the art world (Fresia 2019).

This division of labour has been maintained as a result of a cultural hegemony; a theory originating in Neo-Marxist thought and created by philosopher Antonio Gramsci (Cole 2020). The theory emerged from a classical Marxist belief that the values and beliefs of any society reflect those held by the ruling capitalist class through the mechanism or notion of a 'superstructure' (Cole 2020). Cultural hegemony refers to the elite classes ruling by consent through public and private institutions reinforcing the values and beliefs held by the ruling class (Gramsci 1971; Cole 2020). Thus, the capitalist class of the art world set the precedent of what they deem as 'respectable fine art', while benefitting economically from the labours of the artistic institutions in the top and middle levels of the art market (Gramsci 1971; Fresia 2019). In contrast, artists occupying economically (or/and in terms of status) the lower end of the art market (must try and) survive on or below minimum wage earnings through often other low-skilled jobs (and often multiple ones) just to make ends meet (Throsby 1994). What is more, this demographic has little to no agency in the art sphere, resulting in a lack of market share in an unregulated, decentralised and unorganised market where the large number of artists to the small collection of buyers makes achieving those important sales elusive (Throsby 1994; Fresia 2019). The importance of the role of the artists within the lowest social strata of the art world and their role in the unsustainability of the art world is returned to later in this section. These individuals will be referred to as 'low-level' artists as this is how they are referred to in the existing literature.

The ruling capitalist class within this context constitute the upper echelon of high art society; they are the individuals who are seen to do the mental work (Cole 2020; Gramsci 1971). The bosses who hold positions of prestige, such as businesspeople, and directors of large institutions; they sit on the boards of respected galleries or museums, or they are what has come to be known as 'executive' or 'inside artists' (Fresia 2019). 'Inside artists' are essentially those chosen by the elite to represent the art world and uphold the values of the ruling class (Fresia 2019; Lears 1985). An example of the ruling class exerting their cultural pressure over artistic direction was the careful crafting of the group of artists that became known as the 'Abstract Expressionists'. This collective was the frontier in guiding the ideological needs of this emerging hegemonic class post-WWII (Fresia 2019). The Abstract expressionists were politically silent, and therefore did not challenge ruling class ideals; accordingly, they can be seen as (having been) an essential tool in upholding the ruling classes cultural hegemony (Fresia 2019; Cole 2020).

In addition to the ruling class pushing for the art world to be apolitical and not to strive for cultural change, they are complicit in encouraging unsustainable behaviour due to their primary concern being the generation of economic capital (Bates 1975). As a result of this they allow some of the most polluting industries, such as companies like BP or Shell, to be directly affiliated with prestigious art institutions (Mumford 2016). Up until 2022 the National Portrait Gallery in London was sponsored by BP and even had an award titled the BP Portrait Award (Harris 2022). This highlights a really core idea that the elite classes of high art society are not simply unconcerned by the climate crisis but are benefitting from it as a result of being so ingrained in the capitalist economy. In addition to this, Shell scientists have collaborated with the Van Gogh Museum in Amsterdam, The Netherlands to slow the fading of the oil paintings (Shell 2022). This calls attention to polluting industries using their large capital reserves to greenwash their operations. As through associating themselves with the conservation of artworks, they gain a positive public perception for engaging with the protection of art works (ClientEarth 2022). In this study, the term 'Greenwashing' is defined as the selective disclosure of positive information without full disclosure of negative information as to create an overly positive image regarding sustainability and environmental degradation (Lyon & Maxwell 2011).

Together, this elite are the individuals who dictate over the top and middle levels of the art market, represented by (1) the international market which includes major auction houses which account for the largest players, (2) art markets located in regional creative hubs such as Sydney or London (Throsby 1994). Artists operating within these prestigious markets really adopted the capitalist mode of production during the 1960s, where self-proclaimed 'executive artists' were embracing a factory model for making their work (Throsby 1994). Blue-collar artists operating in the lowest level of the art market were employed to manufacture art works in the form of a Fordist production line (Fresia 2019). This factory model capitalises on the use of machinery and the division of labour (Gill & Patt 2008). Therefore, having dire impacts on environmental health through the release of air pollution and the depletion of finite raw materials (Lears 1985). The degradation caused by the production and exhibition of art is discussed in further detail in the next section.

Moreover, Gramsci discussed the

importance of the 'common sense' in the upkeep of a cultural hegemony in his work 'The Study of Philosophy'. A common-sense concept that he challenges is that an individual can succeed economically if they just/purely try hard enough (Gramsci 1971; Lears 1985; Bates 1975). This belief is upheld by the cultural hegemony within the art sphere of capitalism. The elite class pushes the narrative that hard work and determination will bring you economic good fortune and artistic success, perhaps with an emphasis on artistic success in order to not alienate socialist types. Therefore, this is seen as normalising the economic exploitation of low-level artists by the creative industry; as well as in other industries that artists find themselves employed in to supplement their income (Throsby 1994; Cole 2020). Additionally, and this is where things differ from other economic spheres, this economic exploitation of the less appreciated and monetised artist significantly reduces the amount of time they can dedicate to improving and honing an artistic practise (Throsby 1994; Espinosa 2022).

Consequently, proletarian low-status artists cannot or at least struggle to make work regarding the climate crisis with the aim of raising awareness and improving our ability, as individuals and as a society, to be reactive. This is a consequence of the Bourgeoisie of the art world controlling the general direction lower artists should be taking in order to ascend through the three levels of art market (Throsby 1994). Additionally, the cultural hegemony of the art sphere has a psychological and behavioural impact on lower-level artists; the ruling class belief that sustainability is not something to be prioritised results in the over-production of art for art's sake, made from unsustainable materials. Whereas if sustainability was encouraged by the ruling classes, the art paradigm could look a lot different. Therefore, due to a lack of incentive to make work regarding societies' salient problems, artworks of this kind should (theoretically) not exist in great numbers within the top two tiers of the markets. This is due to there not being much chance of personal gain, through economic or artistic reward (Throsby 1994; Fresia 2019).

Ecological Damage of the Art World

The paradoxical relationship between the environmental impacts of the creation, exhibition and attraction of artworks and their intellectual message is a troubling one (Nelson 2014). The methods and mediums which artists use to make their work impact on how sustainable each piece is. The following section will be analysing specific artistic supplies and mediums that are particularly unsustainable, in order to highlight the reality of the damaging effects of artwork on the planet and societies.

Metal work

Firstly, the extraction of metal as a raw material is damaging to the environment through the production of air pollution and the disfiguration of the landscape where the metal ore is found (Sinnett et al. 2020). Metals experiencing high demand are predicted to degrade high-risk environments more readily, as well as disturb more land in order to meet these societal demands (Luckeneder et al 2021; Lebre et al 2020). Of course, this demand does not originate in the demand for metal as an artistic medium; to suggest so would be ludicrous. However, it is important to understand the provenance of the materials being used to create artwork in order to evaluate their sustainability.

Artists may choose to weld when creating work with metal. Welding in this context refers to the sculptural process of connecting two pieces of metal together (Machinery Future 2020). Art pieces made using welding are responsible for producing/emitting harmful gases such as ozone and nitrogen oxides, as well as particulate matter (Golbabaei & Khadem 2015). The release of these chemicals (chemical compounds) in the atmosphere contributes to ecological degradation from the local to the global scale. Nitrous oxide is a particularly potent greenhouse gas, as it is three hundred times more effective at trapping heat in the atmosphere than carbon dioxide (Ng et al 2016). Consequently, welding is not a sustainable practice as it is contributing to processes responsible for climate warming.

Welding produces another harmful gas, ozone. Tropospheric ozone, which is ozone existing in the lower atmosphere is an important greenhouse gas and short-lived air pollutant (CCAC 2022). In addition to its 'global warming' (along with more extreme oscillations of extreme temperatures and winds) effect, ozone also has an impact on the water cycle affecting evaporation rates, cloud formation and therefore precipitation (CCAC 2022).

Casting in metal is also a widely used creative medium; molten metal is poured into a mould cavity where it is then left to solidify. Once cooled, the piece can be extracted from the mould (General Kinematics 2020). Foundries are locations where artists can produce their metal cast work on a large scale; an example of this would be Anthony Gormley's foundry in

Hexham, in the North-East of England. Gormley is most famous for his outdoor work such as the Angel of the North, located in Gateshead in the North-East of England or 'Another Place' located on Formby beach in Merseyside in the North-West of England (Gormley 2022). Foundries are a major source of hazardous air pollutants released into the atmosphere (Joshi 2011).

Paint

As such a widely used medium, painters should be more knowledgeable about the products they are using to create their work. Using paints as a medium for artwork is not perceived as damaging as practices involving heavy equipment or that are raw material intensive (Siegle 2012). However, from oil-based paints to acrylic, painting as an artistic medium has some severe sustainability concerns.

Firstly, oil paints are made of a combination of inorganic and synthetic organic pigments and nut oils, usually linseed oil (Stanfield 2022). Linseed oil is the most sustainable component of paint, being derived from the dried and ripened seeds of the flax plant (Stanfield 2022). However, due to the nature of the global capitalist economy the production of linseed oil is an industrial process; it involves many stages, and the use of large equipment which produces greenhouse gases that contribute to global warming (Watson 2018).

In addition to the environmental costs involved in producing linseed oil, synthetic organic pigments are petrochemicals obtained via the distillation of crude oil (Stanfield 2022). Fractional distillation is an energy intensive process which separates the components of crude oil by the length of the hydrocarbon molecules

(Helmenstine 2020). Furthermore, the crude oil industry is a significant emitter of VOCs (Volatile Organic Compounds). VOCs are released during the processing of crude oil. On top of this, VOCs are found in oil-based paints. When these chemicals react with oxygen, they 'oxidise' to form ozone (Burghardt et al 2016). Ozone in turn is a major pollutant responsible for urban smog in the lower atmosphere and if the ozone gases reach the upper atmosphere, they contribute to the ozone layer. This is furthering the impacts of global climate warming (Stanfield 2022; Pollution Issues 2008).

On the surface, acrylic paint may appear to be a more sustainable option for painters who are mindful of their ecological impact (Paiano et al 2021). Acrylic paint is considered non-toxic, and this may be true when referring to its toxicity to humans. However, some components of the product are degrading and leaching to the environment in which they are disposed. For example, propylene glycol which is found in acrylic paints is non-toxic to humans and is often found in food products. Nonetheless, it is extremely degrading to aquatic environments, waterways and soils (Christensen 2018). However, acrylic paints are water-based and therefore do not require an organic solvent to thin them. Due to this, they could be considered more sustainable than oil-based paints as they result in less VOCs being produced from the processing of crude oil (Stansfield 2022).

Ceramics

Deposits of clay used to create ceramic work, forms due to a build-up of alluvial sediment left by flowing floodwater within a river's watershed

(Almeida 2020). Extraction of clay causes significant degradation to the landscape; the removal of vegetation leaves the topsoil vulnerable to erosion, releasing CO_2 into the atmosphere as well as damaging soil health. Soil is an important carbon sink and therefore its ability to store carbon is important for planetary health (Lal 2004). Moreover, if the top layer of soil is washed away by run-off the land can no longer be used for agriculture. Therefore, sites that have been exploited for clay extraction are often abandoned by farmers (Almeida 2020; Schwartz 2014). Consequently, site recovery is low, and the degraded soil continues to emit CO_2 into the atmosphere, contributing to climate warming (Schwartz 2014).

The impacts of the degradation of soil are two-fold; it is unsustainable in terms of the climate crisis and soil degradation reduces our ability to feed the earth's growing population. This is because leached soil can no longer retain nutrients that are essential for growing crops and therefore this drastically reduces crop yield in these locations (Schwartz 2014).

Furthermore, ceramic products then pass through a kiln in order to transform them into their sturdy finished products (Air Environment 2020). Low fire kilns reach averages of 1,000 degrees C whilst high fire kilns reach 1340 degrees C. The ceramics remain in this environment for several hours and with common fuels being coal, wood and gas. This process is degrading to the environment as a result of air pollution from burning these fuels (Abubakar and Sadiq 2018).

Exhibition and Audience

It is not just the creation of products, but their

shipping and exhibition that contributes to unsustainable practices (Nelson 2014). "Everything about the display of art is ecologically costly" (Nelson 2014 pg. 5). This ranges from the stringent temperature controls imposed by galleries to insurance companies that insist on air travel over sea-freight, the movements of visitors and mode of travel for major exhibitions (Nelson 2014). As well as the use of non-reusable exhibition elements and shipping materials (Lescaze 2022; Harris 2019). Pretty much everything that goes into the production of an art exhibition has an environmental cost, and quite often a large one. Sculptor Antony Gormley states that art fairs serve a small proportion of world's population, and therefore the excessive use of raw materials is recklessly wasteful (Harris 2019).

Furthermore, the audience attracted by the high arts are significant contributors to the unsustainability of the art world (McMillan 2020). Fine Art works are typically spatially restricted, therefore requires an audience to be motile in order to consume them (Nelson 2014; Harris 2019). Despite high level pieces often being on international loan between galleries, allowing different cities around the world to access them. The pieces remain stationary in nature, drawing audiences across borders. The methods which the audience use to be present at exhibitions are polluting due to their reliance on fossil-fuel based transportation (Rea 2019). In addition, this demographic of the population is predominantly of the higher classes, their consumption is overly frivolous, and they often disregard the environment in favour of maintaining a lavish lifestyle (Nelson 2014).

Perhaps this highlights the benefits of wealth on those who possess it, as consuming art has been argued to have many (for instance intellectual or emotional) advantageous effects on both the individual and society (Wall et al. 2019). One study for instance found that taking students to visit art galleries can improve their critical thinking skills (Greene et al. 2013). Another highlights that art reflects the society and culture it has been created in. Art cannot be created in a vacuum, therefore consuming creative works encourages respect and understanding across socio-cultural lines (Kumar 2022). However, if the consumption of art benefits individuals and society by expanding people's ability to connect across differences and think critically about the world surely the high-class members of society should be overwhelmed with concern by the environmental crisis? Sadly, this is not the case (Nelson 2014).

How can we explain this continuation of ecologically damaging behaviour among the art world's consumers? Nelson (2014) likens this behaviour to a religious performance being carried out by pilgrims, as the gallery system finds its roots in the aristocratic palaces of Europe. Comparisons can also be drawn between the modern ruling class travelling to consume artworks and aristocratic members of society undertaking the 'Grand Tour' of Europe back in the 18th Century (Kriz 1997). Young aristocrats would essentially carry out an excursion of cultural tourism for a period of up to two years, often they would return with paintings, sculptures and elegant clothing (Towner 1985). Therefore, it could be justified that the fossil-fuel intensive methods of transportation used to be able to view art, is all in the name of providing a quality cultural education for the ruling classes. As well as serving an educational purpose to the upper classes, spaces where art is exhibited, such as galleries, art fairs or major art auction houses /

auctions, are often used by the ruling class as a sophisticated backdrop to impress patrons or close business deals (McMillan 2020). In this scenario, the art is secondary to the purpose of the jaunt to consume it. Furthermore, no matter how it is justified, this excessive fossil fuel use is extremely damaging to ecological systems globally and attention should be paid as to how the ruling classes are transporting themselves around the world to absorb culture.

Pushing back against unsustainability

Still, there are ways the art world is mobilising to reduce its environmental impact. By donating to organisations that 'offset' carbon emissions, this allows the art world to continue to produce and exhibit art at a lessened toll to the Earth. UN Gold Standard verified offsetting projects include forestry and renewable energy. The concept is simple: donate to these initiatives and reduce your net carbon footprint (Slotover 2021; Rea 2019). Donating to these organisations may appear to be aiding in replenishing the earth's ecology / balance at face value. However, when considering the bigger picture issues arise which tarnish the impact of offsetting. On average trees take 30 years to grow to a size where they can sequester a decent amount of carbon and even then, these trees might not survive as a result of deforestation (Slotover 2021). Additionally, carbon offsets have been commodified, voluntary carbon offsets can be sold to companies, public bodies and individuals. The commodified offset is generated from a project that prevents or reduces greenhouse gases (GHG) entering the atmosphere or that capture the GHG emissions. A carbon offset is not a tangible product, there is no real reduction in GHGs happening therefore, this should not be a widespread technique for sustainability within the arts as it is a rubberstamping method of ensuring the business-as-usual model is preserved (Lovell et al 2009).

Therefore, to improve the efficacy of offsetting through donating to emission reduction initiatives arts organisations and galleries are opting for a more effective method of carbon offsetting. An environmental charity called ClientEarth has committed to using the law to push faster action on the principles set out in the 2015 Paris Climate Agreement (Slotover 2021). For example, in 2020 ClientEarth Lawyers won a legal case holding Europe's largest coal power station Belchatow, in Poland, accountable to reduce emissions top zero (Slotover 2021).

Despite the success of environmental charities such as ClientEarth, offsetting is a corporate strategy to 'level out' carbon emissions. However, in order to reach the targets which were set in the 2015 Paris Agreement collectively we must be aiming for zero emissions. Critics say that artists and artists organisations utilising this method of carbon offsetting are operating behind a façade to avoid addressing the real problem (Rea 2019). We are overshooting our planet's boundaries (or ecological footprint), and we're reaching the point of no return in terms of a tipping point or a run-away scenario (Raworth 2017). In other words, the arts world is 'greenwashing' their approach to being sustainable in order to continue with their business-as-usual approach.

Another way the arts is attempting to tackle its unsustainability is through third party charity organisations. An example of this being 'Julie's Bicycle' (Bhatt 2020). They offer free resources to companies looking to reduce their carbon footprint; through collaboration with the arts and cultural sector they aim to mobilise these industries to take action to reduce their contribution to the ecological crisis (Julie's Bicycle 2022; Bhatt 2020). This is being achieved through their consultancy service which they provide to businesses globally, despite it being a London-based enterprise. Additionally, through the Arts Council England (ACE)'s environmental program, a 12% decrease in total energy use emissions was recorded between the 2019/20 period (Julie's Bicycle 2022).

Despite their vision and achievements, Julie's Bicycle has been involved in funding and working with artist Olafur Eliasson to create 'Ice Watch'; an installation artwork that has taken place in Paris in 2015, London in 2018 and in Katowice, Poland in 2018 to coincide with COP24 (Julie' Bicycle

2018). The work in London consisted of 110 tonnes of glacial ice that was taken from the Nuup Kangerlua fjord located outside Nuuk, Greenland (Julie's Bicycle 2018). Julie's Bicycle did state that the apprehension of the ice blocks did not affect the quantity of ice in Greenland (Julie's Bicycle 2018). As the blocks were separate from the ice sheet they were once attached to, a simple understanding of the albedo effect would highlight this to be true (Henderson-Sellers & Hughes 1982). However, the shipping of these ice blocks to Paris and London whilst keeping the ice at temperatures below zero in order to keep the ice in a good condition for the start of the installation would have been incredibly carbon intensive. Perhaps the carbon footprint of this piece is or can be seen as negligible when considering the message, it aimed to convey to its audience. The purpose of 'Ice Watch' was to bring climate change into close contact with the public, the audience(s) were encouraged to touch the ice and take in the urgency of the climate crisis (Julie's Bicycle 2018). This kind of 'protest art' can help put sustained pressure onto governments and the private sector through kick-starting conversations regarding all things climate crisis (Buckingham 2015). Due to the tactile and personal approach the audience are encouraged to take to 'Ice Watch' the artwork emotionally simulates the audience members. Whether this response is positive or negative, art that invokes an emotional response can succeed in making climate change personally relevant and therefore precedes stewardship behaviour (Sommer and Klockner 2021).

Nevertheless, if provoking an emotional response in the public is the secret to mobilising the population to behave in a more climate friendly way (Geiger et al 2017) and there is a wealth of eco- activist and protest art available for consumption by the public, so why are we not seeing large scale changes to public behaviour? Weber (2006) suggests this is because global warming does not scare us (yet?). Negative emotions such as fear are extremely motivating for us to change our behaviour in order to remove ourselves from a dangerous situation. However, the proprietors of the ecological crisis are not exposed to the effects of climate change at the frontline (yet) and do not willingly expose themselves to 'eco-protest art'. They can be cast as being or indeed perhaps are completely unconcerned with how their economic activity damages the environment as long as they continue to make a profit (Cohen 2020).

Accordingly, it is appropriate to ask the question, are organisations like Julie's Bicycle effective in achieving a less carbon intensive arts and culture sector? Or are they (rather) rubber-stamp organisations greenwashing the sustainability of the arts so that artists can continue using polluting mediums and energy intensive methods and (select) audiences can consume that art?

The promise of ecological art

As the climate crisis and rapid unsustainable development continue to have catastrophic impacts, there has been a specific branch of the art world that have found this difficult to ignore (Kagan et al 2014). The practise of 'ecological art' is defined as an umbrella term for other buzzwords within the Fine Art paradigm, such as 'environmental art' or 'land art'. Ecological art works are concerned with ecological restoration and eco-activism (Kagan et al 2014; Thornes

2008). These artworks aim to draw their audience's attention to the interdependence of the earth's systems and how they sustain all life on earth; they are also created using natural and sustainable materials (Demos 1969). In addition to bringing a message of stewardship to their audience, the aim of ecological art is to be intrinsically restorative (Kagan et al 2014). This occurs primarily within land art works, as these pieces exist within the landscape. Therefore, ecological art is concerned with reclaiming and remediating damaged environments as well as promoting sustainable consumption (Kagan et al 2014; Thornes 2008).

Environmental art differs from land art as it can be viewed in a gallery in the form of photography, painting, sculpture and film using both artificial and natural materials (Thornes 2008). An example of this would be 'Pollution Pods' by Michael Pinsky (Pinsky & Sommer 2020).

The work is composed of 5 interconnected geodesic domes that each house an emulation of the air in 5 different cities across the globe: London, New Delhi, Sao Paulo, Trondheim and Beijing (Pinsky & Sommer 2020). The audience can walk through the domes and experience for themselves these environments and how they differ yet also how the installation symbolises how they are all interconnected. 'Pollution Pods' is an artwork that completely relies on its meaning to convey a message about the climate crisis. In contrast, works such as those created by sculptor Aurora Robson are considered activist art. She reclaims plastic pollution to create her works (Espinosa 2022). Robson's work is therefore multi-faceted as she is recycling materials that are harmful to the environment, keeping them out of landfill and away from marine life, as well as conveying a message of sustainability and how beautiful different ecologies are (Espinosa 2022). However, this kind of sculptural work is not as interactive and, therefore, it could be argued that the impact of the piece on the audience is much less emotive and therefore less likely to have any effect on audience behaviour (Geiger et al. 2017; Sommer et al. 2019).

Communicating environmental concerns via the creative sector is arguably more effective than through information campaigns as the public are engaged through stimulating their cognitions and emotions rather than their logic (Sommer et al. 2019). This has a higher chance of catalysing individual behaviours and grass roots movements, as well as promoting higher public acceptance of climate mitigation policies (Geiger et al. 2017). However, when attempting to sway public opinion, and therefore behaviour to create a more beneficial culture for us to achieve climate justice, it is almost impossible to measure the effects of the artworks after the audience members leave the gallery/ exhibiting space (Sommer et al. 2019). As with the case of 'Pollution Pods'; yes, it brings the reality of climate change to the audience and elicits an emotional response - yet it is still relatively unclear to the individual audience members what their part is in creating these negative effects on the climate.

Perhaps for ecological artworks to have a significant effect on their audience and be able to measure this change, the eco-art movement should focus on creating restorative pieces on the local scale, in response to local problems. Thereby the audience interacting with the piece can observe the rewards of their behaviour change and undergo positive reinforcement as a result (Sommer et al. 2019). Consequently, this behaviour change will have the substance to be maintained (Geiger et al. 2017).

Regardless of how effective ecological artworks would be on a local scale, when comparing this to the global art scene, the impact of this type of movement becomes negligible (Nelson 2014; Sommer et al. 2019). This begs the question; how can we push for a more sustainable arts sector? As not all art is ecological art, but all art must be sustainable in order to prevent the worsening of the climate crisis.

Nonetheless, this subsection of Fine Art is crucial to the future of the sustainability of the paradigm. The existence of this type of art highlights the artistic desire to overcome the capitalist structure the art world is encapsulated by; and campaign for not only a more sustainable art sector but also for a more sustainable society (Kagan et al 2014; Fresia 2019; Throsby 1994). Despite this desire to combat the climate crisis, the cultural hegemony held over the arts by the ruling class is an overpowering force that may not allow the ecological/ environmental art movement to hit the mainstream and thus have a real effect on public opinion and behaviour. This is because the 'capitalists' that make up the ruling class within the art world are primarily concerned with the accumulation of capital (Fresia 2019; Cole 2020). They do not want to promote ecological art that could encourage sanctions on polluting industries on which they rely on to maintain their fortune. As a result, sustainable/ ecological art receives no sustained support from large galleries or creative institutions and therefore fails to achieve saliency within the art world due to the threat it poses to profit. Which in turn deters artists from entering the ecological art sphere, as there is a perceived lack of achievement and financial gain (Fresia 2019).

Summary

This literature review has discussed how the ruling classes preside over the art world via their rule legitimated by the consent of the masses. This consent is achieved by the upper classes through the presentation of their values and beliefs as common sense concepts to the lower classes.

Additionally, the ruling classes do not believe that sustainable behaviour is something of merit therefore encourage the latter in order to accumulate economic capital. Unsustainability is practiced through the overproduction of art works and via carbon intensive methods and excessive raw material use. The degrading impacts of various artistic methods and mediums has been outlined in the above chapter, evidencing the catastrophic environmental impacts overproduction of artwork can have. Moreover, techniques being utilised by the art sphere with the aim of reducing their carbon footprint were discussed, carbon offsetting is a flagship method being utilised. However, this method reinforces a business-as-usual attitude to using degrading methods, therefore does not promote sustainable practice. Finally, ecological art as a force for restoration and activism was discussed for its potential to create a shift in the arts and wider society to more sustainable practice and individual behaviour.

Chapter Three:

Methodology

The following chapter outlines how data was collected and analysed with the aim of answering the research questions laid out below. A qualitative methodology was utilised in this research, conducting semi-structured interviews with 6 artists from a range of artistic and personal backgrounds. In addition to this, secondary data was collected via the internet. Secondary data sets consisted of policy documents from Art's Council England, interviews with artists conducted with third parties, and artist statements outlining the provenance of their artists practice and additional information about specific artworks.

Research Questions

The research questions were developed in the earliest stages of this investigation, initial and broad research was carried out in order to gain background knowledge about art and sustainability within the sector. As core arguments and concepts emerged in the literature, the research questions evolved.

> **Q1**. To what extent can Gramsci's theory of cultural hegemony be extrapolated to the arts?

> **Q2**. In terms of the effects of production and consumption of art works, how environmentally sustainable are the Fine arts?

Q3. How far does Gramsci's theory of cultural hegemony explain unsustainability within Fine art?

Q4. How far can ecological art account for a shift towards sustainable behaviour within the arts and in wider society?

Data Collection

Sampling

Non-probability convenience sampling was utilised in order to collect the sample for this study. In the beginning, individual artists were chosen based on non-random characteristics of their work; ecological themes in terms of making and meaning was a priority (Stratton 2021). This was an attempt to collect information regarding ecological art, its meanings and ability to improve sustainability within the arts. However, whilst gathering the sample, it became concerning that the chosen sample could only meaningfully answer one of the research questions posed, concerning why the arts may be unsustainable. Therefore, the sampling frame was expanded in scope to include artists from a wider range of backgrounds. This enabled the researcher to gather a wealth of data that could be analysed to draw conclusions across all four research questions.

Nonetheless, the sample contained a disproportionate number of ecological artists than would typically be found in the wider population of artists. Therefore, results from this data could not be extrapolated to the wider artist population. Nevertheless, results from any investigation gathering participants through convenience sampling cannot be applied to the wider population (Stratton 2021). Thus, the research sample is an advantageous one despite its shortfalls; the researcher was able to gather primary data concerning the ecological arts and their potential, as well as information concerning class mechanisms within the arts from some artists unconcerned with themes of environmental stewardship.

Widening the parameters of the non-random characteristics from ecological artists to artists in general permitted the use of another non-probability sampling technique: snowball sampling. At the end of each semi-structured interview artists were asked if they knew any other artists that would be interested in taking part in an interview. Artists emerged as an elusive population to get in touch with, therefore getting referred to potential participants through friends or colleagues granted the researcher with a better chance of access. The credibility provided by being referred improved the likelihood of getting a further interview (Maynard et al 2011).

Semi-structured interviews

This study's primary data set was collected through semi-structured interviews; performed both online through the University provided 'Microsoft Teams' software, and face-to-face with the participant. 5 formal interviews were conducted with practising artists across various mediums: two photographers, two sculptors and one digital artist. Three participants identified as female and two as male; four were from England and one was from Ukraine. Additionally, one interview was conducted with an individual who is employed in a foundry, making sculptures out of metal for a professional artist. This individual lives in England and is female. All interviews were recorded to be transcribed verbatim and in full.

Advantages of semi-structured interviews

Interviewing is a valuable method for investigating how meanings are constructed within their 'natural'/social settings (Cohen et al 2007). They allow the interviewee to express their own thoughts and feelings on the study's subject matter (Berg, 2007). Cultural hegemony is being utilised as the premise for this study's deductive analysis, it impacts the psychology and behaviour of the individuals within a society ruled by consent (Lears 1985). Therefore, interviews proved an advantageous method for this investigation, as the researcher was able to collect data regarding the artists' personal (dependant on levels of disclosure and trust) and professional lives (Alshenqeeti 2014). The semi- structured interview design is one of flexibility, as the layout of the interview is not uniform as with the structured interview; this allows for follow-up questions, for the interviewee to elaborate and for a rich discussion to ensue (Cohen et al 2007). An inductive analysis was also performed on the primary data, and therefore, semi-structured interviews were the technique best suited to this investigation. Flexibility allowed the formation of a rich and detailed data set providing the ideal springboard to produce themes, codes and concepts (Thomas 2006).

Additionally, with simple organisational tools, such as checklists and timing intervals, the interviews could be on the one hand, structured sufficiently to ensure the interviewer covers relevant topics, essential for conducting a deductive analysis; but on the other hand, not too structured to allow greater freedom of expression and comfortability to the artist being interviewed. Additionally, the interviews were explorative enough to justify an inductive analysis. Therefore, this allowed for an in- depth probing into the knowledge, opinions and feelings of the interviewee whilst keeping the interview on topic and concise (Nowell et al 2017).

Secondary sources

A large proportion of ecological art is not confined to a gallery setting (Kagan 2014). Therefore, artworks are not always accompanied by essays usually found in galleries/ exhibition spaces to accompany and elaborate on the work. As a result, this study also drew upon artist statements and interviews as contextual secondary data; acquired through email correspondence with the artist or their (studio's) website. Ten secondary data sources of this nature were analysed for codes and themes, with five of them being the statements of ecological artists, not interviewed by the researcher. These pieces contained information concerning the provenance of their artistic practice, as well as their personal background. The other five sources were gallery notes/statements concerning ecological artists/artworks.

Middle and high-level artists (in terms of visibility/status and presumably economic success) emerged as an elusive population to interview. Reaching out to over 40 artists and only receiving seven responses, three of which were formal rejections. Therefore, Interviews with artists and artists statements were collected via the internet to gain information on how this population operate in terms of sustainability and their beliefs surrounding their own practice (Long-Sutehall et al 2010). Furthermore, the artists are communicating their beliefs organically which provides a detailed and rich data set; this is advantageous when conducting an inductive analysis as concepts emerge that had not been considered by the researcher, enhancing the set of conclusions the researcher is able to draw (Thomas 2006).

Additionally, the secondary data sets are completely free of interviewer bias (Baldwin et al 2022); when communicating their ideas in this form, the artists were not aware a researcher would be analysing them for themes to answer specific research questions. Nonetheless, the artists or the editors of the secondary data may have had a target audience in mind when creating the content, and therefore may contain bias through converg to the ideology of those most likely to view the art piece/ work of the artist being interviewed. However, there is no way that the interviews or statements are bias towards the specific research questions regarding Gramscian theory; meaning deductive analysis to identify themes of cultural hegemony will form valid conclusion as there is no attempt, even unconsciously to converge their responses with the aims of the study (Galdas 2017). Yet, the inductive analysis carried out to identify patterns in the data set could be affected by this potential bias. Therefore, conclusions drawn from inductive analysis of artists statements and secondary interviews will be compounded with evidence from policy documents and primary interview data to improve the rigour of the conclusions.

Data Analysis

Thematic Analysis

Thematic analysis is a highly flexible method for identifying, organising and reporting themes which present themselves in a qualitative data set (Braun & Clarke 2006; Nowell et al 2017). Once familiar with a data set, the researcher then applies codes to information they deem to be relevant (Kiger and Varpio 2020). Codes are 1–2-word phrases which sum up why the information is relevant to answering the research questions (Kiger and Varpio 2020). The codes are collated and grouped into 3-4 themes which subsequently inform the answers to the research questions (Braun and Clarke 2006). A theme represents something important about the data with reference to the research questions.

Two types of reasoning were applied to three different qualitative data sets in this study. Both are outlined below, alongside justifications and explanations for their respective use.

Deductive reasoning

A deductive, theory-driven approach was used to analyse guidance and policy documents from Arts Council England (ACE) and the UK's Department for Digital, Culture, Media and Sport

(DCMS).

The aim of this analysis was to establish the validity of applying classical Marxism and Gramsci's (Neo- Marxism) theory of cultural hegemony to the way the (fine) arts world operates. This is both in terms of production and consumption, the class struggle connected with / inherent in it, and how this upholds the capitalist culture of unsustainability. Deductive analysis is a useful technique for focusing on a particular feature of data in question that could be best (or at least credibly) understood in the context of cultural hegemony (Braun & Clarke 2006; Hyde 2000). Thus, allowing for the generation of conclusions regarding environmental and social sustainability within the arts. When coding the data, the researcher would concentrate on identifying information that provides evidence that cultural hegemony was a valid theory to conceptualise capitalism in an arts world context. For example, any reference to capital or investment was labelled thematically as 'economic'.

Additionally, the primary interview data set, engaging with artists was also subject to deductive analysis. Again, this was done so as to identify if the application of cultural hegemony is a valid one. The interview data was more specific to the individual artists themselves and their opinions regarding the climate crisis. Therefore, conclusions could be drawn regarding the class structure within the arts. However, this could only inform the study's interest in sustainability on the level of the personal.

Inductive reasoning

Inductive reasoning is a systematic procedure which aims to derive themes, concepts and models from a qualitative data set (Thomas 2006). The technique was used here in order to analyse the interview responses and the ecological artist statements. The specific content of the data is generalised through interpretations made by the researcher. These interpretations evolved into patterns, which provided elicitations in response to the research questions (Weisberger & Bradford 2021). The intention of this analysis was to investigate and reach conclusions concerning how sustainable the arts world is, how seriously sustainability is being considered, and whether ecological art could mitigate sustainability concerns in the arts.

Advantages of Thematic Analysis

The flexibility which accompanies thematic analysis has been the method's primary strength, as the technique is independent from any epistemological or theoretical approach (Tuckett 2004). This allows the researcher to collect a rich and detailed, yet complex, account of data without unnecessary built-in constraints (Braun & Clarke 2006). This method of analysis is not too difficult to understand and relatively straightforward to carry out. Therefore, it is perfect for novice researchers (Neuendorf 2018).

In addition to the ease of use and flexibility of the overall method, the results obtained from a thematic analysis are broadly accessible to the educated public (Braun & Clarke 2006). The applied aim of this research is to start a conversation on figuring out how to make the arts more sustainable; this cannot be achieved without the understanding and support of people within the creative sector. Therefore, the results being accessible greatly increases the chances of the conclusions being used to make real- world changes.

Research Positionality

When conducting research within the social sciences, it is important that the researcher is aware of and declares their respective positionality (Holmes 2020). A research position "refers to a system of beliefs and assumptions about the development of knowledge" (Sanders, 2019 p 130). Intrinsic to the researcher's identity, positionality influences how the research is conducted. Impacting the validity of the outcomes and conclusions (Rowe 2014). Thus, the reader should take note of the researchers position in order to evaluate the robustness of the study's conclusions (Holmes 2020).

This dissertation was conducted from an interpretivist research position. This is informed by a critical realist ontology; dictating that individuals perceive reality through a personalised lens and therefore individual experiences vary significantly due to the inaccuracy of our senses to narrate our own experiences (Stanley & Wise 1993). This can explain the researcher's interest in investigating sustainability through the lens of neo-Marxist theory; Marx encouraged for social phenomena to be interpreted through an epistemically exterior position (Patnaik 2019). In essence, this means striving to understand the world with the intent on changing it for the better (Lyons 2017). Similarly, this investigation has interpreted that the arts are unsustainable and taken research routes to investigate what is being/can be done to improve it.

Furthermore, a Marxist analysis of capitalism reflects core interpretivist beliefs; it is held within this framework that different socio-economic classes are experiencing reality in ways that are completely different from one another. Therefore, both class demographics are experiencing reality separately; the ruling class is legitimising their dominance through consent, whilst the lower classes are providing their consent to at least some degree by internalising ruling class beliefs and values. However, reality is being constructed between them through socio-economic interaction and is defined by class relations. Ontologically, the researcher believes in the existence of an objective truth. However, interpretivist epistemology dictates that reality is created intersubjectively through social interaction and partially shared meanings (Sanders at al 2019). Consequently, this objective truth is not accessible to human researchers. The collection of qualitative interview data reflects this interpretivist position as the information collected is a subjective account of personal experiences; this data is then subject to further subjective analysis by the researcher. Through an interpretivist framework the researcher is an integral part of the research design as they shape the study by incorporating their own values and beliefs (Rogers 2020); highlighting that reality is constructed intersubjectively (Sanders et al 2019).

Limitations

The flagship drawback of this study was the time-consuming nature of the qualitative process. This was particularly challenging when working to a strict deadline, the researcher being a novice and choosing to analyse three large data sets. Additionally, due to the use of secondary sources as well as the semi-structured nature of the (primary) interviews, a lot of the information proved irrelevant to the research questions due to deviance from the main issue being studied or just non-relevance entirely (Leung 2015).

Frequently criticised for lacking scientific rigour due to poor justification and a lack of transparency; qualitative methods have a bad reputation in some positivist circles when it comes to the validity and reliability of the results produced (Noble & Smith 2015). In this type of inquiry, where the researchers own values and beliefs can so easily seep into the findings of the research, close attention needs to be paid to these concepts (Cypress 2017). This is particularly important when this study is being conducted through an interpretivist lens; a belief held by the researcher is that their influence is inevitable (Stanley & Wise 1993). Furthermore, it is difficult to verify results as participants are in control of the information the researcher can collect from them, and one has to assume participants are being trustworthy and reliable narrators of their own experiences (Cypress 2017; England 1994). Therefore, the researcher cannot verify the results against the scenarios that are being discussed, as it is a situation in which the research's observation and scrutiny mode has not experienced / or is unable to experience in that exact setting, in an objective fashion itself (Leung 2015).

In addition, replicating qualitative investigations is a difficult task as the basis of the research is the acquisition of opinions and judgements from the sample, which cannot be analysed mathematically (Sharma 2017). Consequently, ensuring results are accurate or representative is difficult to test.

Notwithstanding some of the difficulties involved in conducting a piece of qualitative research, this methodology is best suited to this present study as it is investigating how individual behaviour fits into a larger economic system (capitalism), and how this does or can generate unsustainable behaviour. It would be difficult to design a study, in the time frame available to objectively measure this. Additionally, this research tackled the subject of ecological art and if this can generate positive change within the arts. In order to gain an insight into this topic, the research had to collect information pertaining to opinions, beliefs and values.

Concerns regarding the replicability of conclusions drawn from thematic analysis emerged as a limitation within this research. The method is very flexible, which can generate criticism for it not being robust enough (Kiger and Varpio 2020). The flexibility could potentially also lead to inconsistency and a lack of coherence (Nowell et al 2017), particularly when being conducted by a novice researcher (Cypress 2017). Even when the technique is performed to a high standard, the researcher is influencing the analysis through applying their own belief system to the information. This present research addresses this as a core part of the generation of knowledge as it has been conducted through an interpretivist lens (Sanders et al. 2019). Therefore, thematic analysis is an appropriate technique to have used in this study, as it is concerned with generating further understanding of an intersubjective reality concerning what drives non-sustainability in the arts.

Finally, constraints on the nature of the sample surfaced as a result of the combined use of two non- probability sampling techniques: convenience and snowballing. One major disadvantage of using non- probability sampling overall is that it is not possible to find out how well you were representing the wider population within your sample (Sharma 2017). Therefore, the accuracy of your results could be called into question, as the conclusions drawn from the data cannot be accurately extrapolated to the target population (Berndt 2020).

Convenience sampling could be influenced by researcher bias. In order to collect a large amount of the sample (relatively) quickly, the researcher may learn what kind of individual will agree to participate (Berndt 2020). Additionally, convenience sampling does not try to systematically identify sub-groups with a target population (Sharma 2017). Therefore, potential differences that arise in participant characteristics or results from their data cannot be explored systematically or explained (Stratton 2021). Furthermore, snowballing sampling could generate a bias sample, as being referred to individuals by existing participants has the potential to create a sample sharing similar traits. Despite the drawbacks of the sampling techniques utilised in this investigation with the resources available to the present researcher these methods were the ones most suitable to the research aims.

Summary

Within the methodology chapter the merits, shortfalls and mitigation steps taken have been discussed to allow the robustness of this study to be evaluated by the reader. The methods utilised in this investigation provide a high level of rigour as mitigation was taken against bias by widening the sampling frame when it became clear its parameters were too stringent to collect a representative sample. Additionally, major advantages of this method include: the use of semi- structured interviews facilitating the collection of a rich data set, enabling analysis via inductive and deductive reasoning. As a result of this, analysis could support answers to all four research questions.

Finally, the flexibility of thematic analysis provided a processed data set that remained rich in detail and nuance.

Chapter Four:

Findings and Discussion

This chapter will present the findings extrapolated from the data sets whilst incorporating literature referenced in chapter two, as well as expanding into unexplored literature to support the subsequent discussion. The following chapter will be split up into four sections corresponding with the four themes that have emerged from the analysis of primary and secondary data sources.

Cultural hegemony in the arts

Analysis of policy documents supported the application of Gramsci's theory of cultural hegemony to how the art world and creative sector operates economically. Discussion within the documents focused on ideas of promoting economic growth within cultural institutions through achieving an increased amount of "public, private and commercial investment" specifically in culture and creativity by 2030 (Arts Council England 2020). The ACE 'Let's Create' strategy promotes green economic growth, as the basis to establish a culture of sustainability within the creative sector. This is put forward as a common-sense concept. As discussed in chapter two, appealing to the common- sense of the proletariat is a tool of the ruling class, used to embed their values and beliefs into wider society. When previously discussed, the importance of common sense within the upkeep of a cultural hegemony, was concerned with individuals not necessarily being guaranteed economic success despite working hard (Lears 1985). Conversely, the policy documents suggest that the cultural hegemony enforcing unsustainable practice is upheld by promoting that the phenomenon creating negative social and environmental effects is the obvious solution to sustainability problems within the arts.

Moreover, ACE's strategy argues that through community engagement, economic growth and an emphasis on inclusivity and representation, a higher degree of sustainability can be achieved in the creative sector (Arts Council England 2020. However, the document provides no details on how this will be done except through "promoting research and development and supporting the adoption of new technologies" (Arts Council

England 2020 pg. 23) This supports the observation that economic growth is being exploited as a common-sense belief as no evidence has been provided in the document on how sustainability will be achieved.

Furthermore, this is an example of greenwashing and rubberstamping by the art worlds ruling class; with the aim of maintaining a business-as-usual approach to how it operates. This is a mechanism of the cultural hegemony as the promotion of economic growth within the creative sector, green or not, will benefit the ruling classes through the creation of capital. Accordingly, despite any degrading socio-environmental impacts green economic growth will continue to prevail as a solution to unsustainability as the ruling classes with remain steadfast in their role.

Additionally, the contents of one ACE report analysed titled 'How to quantify the public benefit of your Art Gallery using value estimates' discusses how to extrapolate cultural value using an economic framework (Lawton et al 2021). The core aim of the guidance document is to "estimate in monetary terms the value held by society that is not captured in existing economic measures" (Lawton et a 2021). Including access fees or economic spend by visitors or users; this highlights the need for the ruling classes in the art world to commodify culture in order to reveal its worth in an economic context. Emphasised in chapter two, the art world is inherently economic due to the value ascribed to art works as financial assets (Throsby 1994). Furthermore, it is revealed in the ACE guidance document that the arts are commodified to the extent that even cultural experiences are to be assigned an economic value. Illuminating how submerged within the capitalist economy the arts are. Therefore, commodification is a tool used by the ruling classes to uphold the cultural hegemony; supporting the idea explored in chapter two, that art and the experiences it provides are economic products. They can be bought, sold and retained (Throsby 1994).

Primary interview responses further support that the commodification of the arts occurs to uphold the cultural hegemony of the ruling class. Both high-level and low-level artist participants reported that they felt a pressure to produce artworks continuously in order to become or continue to be a successful artist. As referred to in chapter two, this commodification is not classically capitalist, yet in the interviews it became clear that artists are mass producing work with the hope of it being mass consumed. Here mass consumption does not exclusively refer to being bought but, being viewed whether that be online or in person. The prevailing reason given for this was feelings of inadequacy due to other "Artists appearing to be making an artwork a day" on social media. P6 claimed that they "think Instagram puts a lot of pressure on the art world" to continually produce work. In addition to this, 5/6 participants reported that they feel that an obvious class divide exists within the art world. Expression through generalised comments like "Wealthier artists have more opportunities" to more personal and pitiful declarations of "Often (artists) are left to choose between materials and paying rent."

This encapsulates the essence of a Gramscian cultural hegemony, as artists have internalised the 'common-sense' belief that if they work hard enough, produce enough, they will be able to subsist as a successful artist (Gramsci 1971; Lears 1985). However, they also acknowledge that constraints exist, intrinsic to the capitalist system that make this impossible for some (Lears 1985).

Therefore, the class divide within the arts puts pressure on high and low-level artists to overproduce their works. This contributes to an unsustainable culture within the art world as in order to over produce there is an excessive use of raw materials (Wiedmann et al 2020).

On top of the evidence gathered from primary interviews, the artist statements and secondary interviews with high-level artists carry connation's of high personal or family wealth. Providing further evidence for the class divide within the arts; as this insinuates that high-level artists, in other words, those who practice art as well as being able to subsist from being an artist are from wealthier backgrounds. Therefore, to be successful in the creative sector, wealth is a prerequisite (Cascone 2019). This is a function of the capitalist system as the ruling class of the wider economy take their place as the ruling class of the art sphere, this is supported by primary interview data as P5 stated that wealthier artists "have better financial support structures in order to take risks." The implication here is that individuals practicing art are better able to evolve into professional artists as they have excess time and resources to commit to honing their artistic skills and practice. This is supported by P1 stating that "Being able to study art is ultimately a privileged position to be in as we have time to sit and contemplate art."

In addition to being able to hone their artistic skills and ponder intellectual meanings and aesthetic design, P2 expressed concern for the lack of "opportunities for training whilst on the job, so a degree is necessary." What's more is that P4 affirmed that existing as an artist is difficult so "unless you have ways of supporting yourself by other means, it's a major challenge to exist as an artist."

In reference to sustainability, cultural hegemony is sustained through the beliefs and values of the ruling class being presented as common-sense concepts that the lower classes must accept (Lears 1985). The prevailing example that emerged from the primary and secondary data is that lower-level artists must work hard in order to achieve artistic and economic success. However, due to constraints built-in to the capitalist system, most are unable to transcend their original strata specifically within the art world. This idea encourages the unsustainable practice within the creative sector as artists feel societal and economic pressure to continuously over produce their work in order to remain relevant and for their product to be consumed. This utilizes an unnecessary excess of raw materials; for no other reason than to remain relevant. P4 described "often having to step back and ask myself why I'm making work" when they get caught up in the culture of mass production.

Furthermore, secondary interview data revealed that high-level artists are also complicit in the upkeep of the cultural hegemony. Larger studios run by professional artists, particularly those practicing ecological arts, have discussed the benefits of micro-actions in combatting their own sustainability shortfalls. In an interview obtained through correspondence with Olafur Eliason's studio, in Germany. It was reported the studio practices sustainability through micro-actions such as having a completely plant-based kitchen and using 100% recycled paper (Eliasson et al 2020). On the surface, these actions appear advantageous, artists are taking responsibility for their mass production and countering this by switching to a more environmentally friendly alternatives of consumption. However, the promotion of micro-actions is aiding the upkeep of the cultural hegemony, contributing to the unsustainability of art. High-level artists focusing on creating small scale shifts in their consumption does not attempt to address the systematic constraints in place that drives unsustainability among artists.

Moreover, advocating for micro-actions as a solution to unsustainability is a greenwashing technique that allows for a business-as-usual model to prevail. This is supported by evidence from the same secondary interview where Eliason admits to having no plans on changing the way they make work to make it more sustainable. However, he defends this by stating that "I wouldn't make a good decision for the climate that leads to a bad artistic outcome" (Eliason et al 2020 pg. 147). Despite this statement making sense logically and is supported by P1 expressing that artists are indeed "artists not environmentalists". This is a clear hypocrisy within the arts regarding sustainability, all three data sets have expressed a large concern for the climate crisis; however, when it comes down to individual artistic success and economic gain artists quickly change this narrative to defending their unsustainable practice. This study attributes this to the cultural hegemony reigning over the art world, individuals are aware and concerned by the climate crisis. However, artists adopt this individualist mindset that is innate to economic success in the capitalist system (Lynch et al 2018).

Resulting in them adopting a conflicting mentality of having deep concern for the climate crisis but behaving in a way that exacerbates environmental degradation in pursuit of economic and artistic success.

Environmental Stewardship in a Carbon Intensive Sector
A juxtaposition currently exists between the

intellectual messages of art works and their environmental impacts (Nelson 2014). The intellect behind the work does not have to be directly related to the climate crisis or environmental degradation for this to be a troubling contrast. As art works encouraging the audience to contemplate any intellectual meaning or even just to ponder on the beauty of an object, person or place, should be concerned about their environmental effects. As to consider complex and urgent issues within the realm of the intellect and aesthetic should converge with a decent level of socio-environmental stewardship.

Interdependence surfaced as a core concept within artist statements and secondary interview data; within Carolina Caycedo's artist statement she refers to interdependence as being a fundamental element of her practice. She wants her audience to "understand nature not as a resource to be exploited, but as a living and spiritual entity that unites people beyond borders." Additionally, in an interview with Kumi Naidoo, activist and former Secretary-General of Amnesty International, artist Olafur Eliason explains how he wanted to convey interdependence through his work 'Ice Watch' by helping the audience recognise that 'we are part of this huge unruly network called Earth and our mark, our carbon footprint, on Earth is real and the consequences are real.'

This appreciation for interdependence on Earth highlights the environmental stewardship held by artists occupying the highest level of the art market. This is juxtaposed with an absence of concern for interdependence from the primary interview data set. Artists interviewed by the researcher were more concerned with carbon footprints and their eco depression than the connectivity of Earth systems. P1 went as far to state that they cannot think about the climate crisis for too long without wanting to "Curl up into a ball and cry." This study attributes this to higher level artists having more time and resources to spend on contemplating the climate crisis in full, whereas lower-level artists do not have the mental space to reflect on societies issues due to the situation they find themselves in under capitalism. As explored in chapter two, low level artists struggle economically to subsist as artists and therefore, find themselves occupying minimum wage, low-skilled roles in order to survive (Fresia 2019). Occupying time, they would have been using to contemplate art, on meeting the bottom line (Throsby 1994). Therefore, it is not that low level artists are less concerned about the socio-environmentally degrading effects of interdependence, it is that they do not have the spare mental space to contemplate these problems in relation to their artistic practice.

Moreover, discussion on how this is being achieved had a particular emphasis on the urgency of the situation. An urgency to act in a more sustainable manner to ease the effects of climate change to ensure a future for the planet. This is highlighted by P5 declaring they "Think we are much further away from solving this global crisis than most people care to realize - and we are probably heading towards a mass extinction event" and P1 stated that "I don't think there's long before we push the planet past the point of no return". This urgency is revealed in secondary data sources as Eliasson confronts the idea that 'Our actions today will shape the course of the next decade'; as well as in policy documents, ACE's 'Let's Create' Strategy refers to an 'urgent crisis of climate change and environmental degradation'. In addition to expressing urgency, the strategy also refers to these phenomena as 'the key forces shaping our social, political and economic landscape over the decade to come'. This insinuates that the ruling classes do have a significant interest in approaching the topic of unsustainability within the arts. ACE is a national development organization and therefore has the agency to fund and get sustainable projects off the ground. However, this study argues that the ruling classes do not actually have an interest in promoting sustainability in the arts and the appearance that they do is detrimental to sustainability. This will be discussed in full, in the following section of discussion.

Furthermore, concern for the ongoing climate crisis compounded with support for sustainability and protecting the planet was salient in all three data sets. This concern was discussed in relation to how the arts operate economically, the actual making of work, and regarding wider societal issues with production and consumption. Additionally, it emerged that most participants (5/6) aim to make themes of environmental stewardship intrinsic to how they make work and to the meaning of that work. A particular emphasis on ensuring the individual artist was doing all they could to be sustainable surfaced in the data. P1 noted that they "like working with metal for the fact it can be melted down and recycled," P4 supports this further by claiming that sustainability is at "the core of everything (they) do" as an artist. What's more is that P2 revealed that they have changed their "diet, modes of transport and other forms of consumption …. to be more environmentally friendly" due to concern for the climate crisis and therefore it only "makes sense... to apply it to... (their) artistic practice." Highlighting that artists are distressed regarding the impacts of the climate crisis and are taking some form of responsibility for the effects of their actions both personally and artistically. Further support for this claim comes from P6 stating they "try to buy new cameras less frequently and have (an) electric car also to reduce my carbon footprint. I also place orders for printing my images in Carbon Neutral Laboratories". Additionally, it was expressed in secondary interview data that there is a push to explore carbon neutral alternatives to everyday activities, such as switching meetings online to reduce transport emissions (Eliasson et al 2020).

Ultimately, the disruption of damaging individual consumption patterns is not a fix to the institutional processes that drive over-consumption within the capitalist model of the economy (Anantharaman 2018). Primary interview responses divulged that respondents were aware of the constraints preventing their individual action from having a positive impact on mitigating the climate crisis. P4 disclosed that they "just don't think many artists would be able to realise a fully sustainable practice without professional advice". P1 adds to this by expressing that "we're artists not environmentalists" and when functioning in a system as complex as capitalism it is hard to know what consequences our actions have on sustainability due to interdependence and greenwashing. As P1 articulated it "it sometimes feels like you can't win".

Ecological Art and Behaviour Change

The paradigm of ecological art emerged as a form of ecological activism and a method of raising awareness about the climate crisis (Kagan et al 2014; Thornes 2008). Therefore, this study wanted to investigate if eco art is achieving its aims and how operating under a cultural hegemony impacts its function. Primary interview responses suggest that artists believe that ecological art has the ability to change the mentality and behaviour of its audience. P6 expressed that "art that makes a deep impression will certainly change a person's worldview", P4 stated they feel ecological art works have "influenced the work I do today and increased my need to learn and do more within human rights." Additionally, P5 disclosed that "The arts consider these increasingly urgent issues in sensitive and complex ways. I feel this contributes to a positive change in our understanding and interconnectedness with the environment."

However, responses were mixed with other artists revealing they do not believe ecological art works could have a lasting impact on how their audience think and behave regarding sustainability. P3 states that "a person cannot immediately take and change his behaviour in one moment." P3 elaborated by expressing that "First, the worldview changes, and then the behaviour of a person is possible" but this cannot be done by art works alone, they are the supplementary material. Therefore, it remained unclear whether ecological art works had any positive effect on the arts or on society regarding a switch to sustainable practice.

This study does not attempt to measure the direct impact of ecological art on its audiences as research into how art effects individual behaviour after they have consumed the artwork, specifically highlights this as a difficult task. That cannot be achieved with a degree of certainty (Sommer et al 2019).

Through the study of cultural hegemony and its subsequent application to the art world in this investigation, it appears unlikely that ecological art could flourish as a method of restoration and activism under capitalism; as the themes portrayed within ecological art do not converge with the beliefs and values of the ruling classes. As referenced in chapter two the ruling classes of the art sphere includes businesspeople, directors of large institutions and 'executive' or 'inside' artists (Fresia 2019). Evidence presented in the first section of this chapter 'Cultural hegemony in the arts' suggests that the ruling class of wider society assume their position as the upper echelon of the art sphere due to connation's of personal and family wealth being abundant in secondary interviews and artist statements. Therefore, this form of art which protests the effects of capitalism whilst the system is still generating profit for the ruling class, could not ascend to saliency within the art paradigm. In accordance with the theory of cultural hegemony.

In contrast, there is a wealth of ecological art that is being produced and consumed globally. From seminal pieces such as 'Spiral Jetty' by Robert

Smithson or more contemporary art works such as Aurora Robson's 'Troika.' Accordingly, this study identifies the rise of ecological art as a counterhegemony within the art world. Hegemonies exist on a continuum from open to closed in terms of their flexibility. This research argues that the hegemony over the arts is of the open kind as the potential for resistance has flourished in the form of ecological artwork (Lears 1985). This can be attributed to a rich culture of activism and an urge to create positive change within the arts by those who create and by those who consume (McPherson & Mazza 2014). This has been evidenced in primary interview responses with artists sharing how they have changed their lifestyles and adopted different techniques or mediums to reduce their own carbon footprint. In addition to primary data, secondary sources provided confirmation that it is not just artists and art consumers who are concerned about the climate and want to take positive action but that cultural institutions are searching for solutions to their carbon intensive operations. Arts Council England works with "a core group of arts organisations, museums and libraries, ranging in size and location" to improve their sustainability. Gramsci understood counterhegemonies as the way culture collaborates with the socio-economic constraints of the less powerful (Lears 1985), this can be observed in ecological art as the activities that are being protested within these art works are both harmful to the lower classes socially, economically and environmentally and the ruling classes continue to bring in a profit from them.

Ecological art as a counterhegemony can be understood through Carolina Caycedo's 'Land of Friends' on display at BALTIC: Gateshead between 28 May 2022- 29 January 2023. The work is rich in themes of environmental stewardship and activism, featuring 'communities impacted by large-scale infrastructure and other extraction projects' through 'video, performance, sculpture, installation and drawing'. The BALTIC is a large cultural institution in the North-East of England, hosting the work of 'executive' and 'high-level' artists from around the world. Therefore, hosting an artist that is approaching ecological themes and allowing an audience to contemplate these environmental and social issues insinuates high level art institutions are concerned with issues of sustainability and ecological wellbeing.

Nonetheless, ecological art as a method of activism, and communication with the ruling classes of both the art sphere, and wider society is not plausible under culture hegemony. Due to the rising concern regarding the impacts of climate change globally; it is important that the upper class appear to be engaging with the problem. This is surely a good thing? If the ruling class are engaging with art activists, through funding or the commission of exhibitions. This puts us on the right path to finding sustainable solutions, right? However, secondary interview data suggests this may not be the case, Kumi Naidoo emphasises that a lot of activism mistakes having 'access for (having an) influence' on the ruling class. His critique goes on to state that activists 'spend too much time working towards gaining access to people in power to talk to them about what they already know'. Accordingly, the upper classes are already educated on the impacts of unsustainable behaviour yet are unconcerned to act against the causes of environmental degradation as this will negatively impact them individually (Wiedmann et al 2020). Whether this be through diminished support from stakeholders or reduction in profits by reducing a company or even a sectors emissions or pollution, there is a lot to gain economically from overproduction and therefore the ruling class do not want to change their behaviour (Kettell 2006).

In addition to art activists mistaking access to the ruling class as having a degree of influence over them, the same can be said for having access to an audience. Ecological art and art in general tend to attract the same demographic of people, those who are aware of the impacts of degradation and climate change and are intrigued to learn more or simply reinforce their own views through a creative medium (Kang 2010). This is evidenced in a secondary source, ACE 'Arts Audience: Insights' they found that individuals who are highly qualified, highly affluent and in the early stages of their career were the most engaged with the arts. This demographic is highly educated on social, political and environmental issues of their time and are engaged with ecological art in order to contemplate these issues in a creative context. In the same way the ruling class are already educated on issues of sustainability, attracting an audience that is already fully aware of the devasting impacts of environmental degradation, will have a negligible impact on consumption patterns within wider society. Accordingly, ecological art is not a feasible counterhegemony, to encourage sustainable behaviour within the arts and within society. This is due to the intellectual messages delivered through eco art are gatekept by their existence within echo chambers, and the constraints of capitalism preventing individual consumers having any impact over the system of production (Kettell 2006).

Also revealed in primary interviews was that the inability of individual artists to have influence over their own carbon footprint left them frustrated. Participants discussed how they felt, despite having access to more sustainable materials to create with, these products still had significant sustainability shortfalls. P1 stated that they are "Paying for natural materials to be delivered to (their) home as (they) don't have access to a quarry, it sometimes feels like you can't win" and consequently, they are not having the influence they wanted, which was to find a less carbon intensive way of working. Therefore, positive changes in behaviour regarding sustainability cannot be effectively encouraged by activism through ecological art. In the interview with Kumi Naidoo he described a cultural hegemony where the ruling classes provide activists with access as a method of greenwashing their reputation. However, in terms of eco art the ruling classes allow the artists with access to an audience, whether this be commissioning an exhibition or providing funding for a work; knowing that the society in which the audience lives provides no option to be truly sustainable in their consumption. Highlighted in ACE 'Let's Create' with an emphasis on reaching larger audiences in order to expose more viewers to the influential art of the decade. This study argues that the only reason ecological art can exist as a counterhegemony is because the potential of the work influencing the audience's behaviour is negligible and unthreatening to the hegemony itself, as any individual change in consumption means nothing within the constraints of capitalism.

Summary

The contents of this chapter has laid out the findings of this study and explored them within the context of the wider literature. The data supports that the arts are deeply concerned by the ongoing climate emergency, however engagement in environmentally degrading behaviours in relation to artistic practice is prevalent. This is evidenced across responses from primary interview participants and artists expressing their views through secondary data. The main reason attributed for this juxtaposition is the internalisation of the belief that sustainability is not of prime concern to artists, and that they should continue to produce work despite degrading consequences. This belief originates as one of the ruling classes and this internalisation is an essential process in the maintenance of a cultural hegemony.

Victoria Slattery

Chapter Five:

Conclusion and Recommendations

The purpose of this research was to investigate if the theory of cultural hegemony could be applied to the arts and how this impacted the ability of the discipline to be sustainable in its practice. Also studied was the potential of ecological art as a method through which the arts could stimulate sustainable practice within the discipline, as well as generate momentum to create change within wider society towards a more sustainable modus operandi.

Through the analysis of primary interview data, collected by the researcher, alongside secondary data consisting of policy documents from ACE and interviews with artists accompanied by statements of ecological artists regarding the provenance and meaning of their work; this dissertation has revealed that Gramscian cultural hegemony is a reasonable premise to apply to the art sphere of society. Most participants felt there is a noticeable class divide within the arts, this divide was also evidenced in artist statements through conations of personal wealth leading to artistic success. This resulted in the finding that the ruling class of society take on the role of the ruling class within the arts. Therefore, they rule through gaining the consent of the lower classes by instilling their values and beliefs into them as 'common-sense.' Capitalist common sense assumes that in order to be successful there must be an overproduced commodity that can be overconsumed to generate economic capital; the commodification of the arts as objects and experiences evidenced in ACE documents, conveys how far the arts is embedded into the capitalist structure. Furthermore, the arts functions as a microcosm of capitalism. Through the internalisation of the pseudo common- sense belief that if they work hard enough, they will succeed, lower class artists overproduce their work to such a degree that they believe they can achieve artistic and economic success. However, the internal constraints of wider capitalism results in the lower classes of the art sphere being exploited as a member of the labour force. Due to their lower economic status, they must undertake low income, low skilled roles in order to survive and sacrifice their arts practice in favour of economic work.

Moreover, an essential element of the existence of a cultural hegemony is the upkeep of the ruling classes rule by consent. Business-as-usual is reinforced through the ruling classes support for a shift to more sustainable practice within the discipline. Evidenced in ACE documents which state an aim to achieve a higher degree of sustainability in the arts yet when providing context to how this will be achieved, the policy claims that green economic growth is the most reliable route. However, this is another common-sense view of the ruling class that is internalised by the lower classes to prevent a shift to sustainability. The ruling class aim to maintain a business-as-usual model, as in the wider economy mass production and consumption leads to the accumulation of economic capital.

Therefore, the cultural hegemony overseeing the arts, is impacting the disciplines' ability to be sustainable. Artist participants declared that they believe overproduction is a genuine problem within the arts, citing social media and the pressure of remaining relevant as the main causes of this behaviour. This overproduction in the arts, just like in the wider economy, is the root of the disciplines unsustainable practice. As previously discussed, this overproduction originates in the function of the cultural hegemony. Artists believe the ascension to success is through the overproduction of their work, to be mass consumed by an audience through the sale of an artistic commodity, attendance to an exhibition/gallery or consumption of artistic content online. However, the creation, exhibition and attraction of an audience to consume artworks are carbon intensive processes with environmentally degrading consequences.

Thus, this investigation inquired into the relevance of ecological art within the sustainability of arts. Ecological art sets out to make environmental stewardship a core element of the creation and meaning of the artwork, with the aim of sharing this message with its audience. Participating artists were divided in their opinions on how well ecological art can encourage sustainable behaviour both within the discipline and in its audience. Nevertheless, this research deduced that ecological art exists as a counterhegemony to the hegemony of the ruling class; therefore, ecological artists and their audiences are permitted to engage in art activism and discuss issues of sustainability under the cultural hegemony. However, this is only allowed due to the ruling class having preconceived that ecological art will have little to no influence on their ability to maintain a business-as-usual approach to production and consumption.

Finally, ecological art will not have a positive impact on sustainability within the arts or in wider society as in order to reduce the environmental degradation as a result of production in both the arts and wider society, major adjustments are needed in the way artists and the public consume.

However, sustainable consumption within the capitalist model is an extremely difficult task due to the complexities of interdependence, individuals can never be completely certain they have made a sustainable choice.

To summarise, a cultural hegemony presides over the arts creating a culture where unsustainable practice is accepted as business-as-usual. The environmentally degrading impacts of the creation, transportation, exhibition and of attracting an audience to the art works is upheld by the ruling class as consumption of artistic commodities facilitates the accumulation of economic capital.

Victoria Slattery

References

Abubakar, E and Sadiq, Y.O (2018) 'The Potential of Biogas as Fuel for High Temperature Ceramic Kiln Firing.' Journal of the Environment. December. 12(2).

Almedia, J (2022) ENVIRONMENTAL IMPACTS CAUSED BY CLAY EXTRACTION IN THE MUNICIPALITY OF BIASSUCÊ-BA.

Alshenqeeti, H (2014) 'Interviewing as a Data Collection Method: A Critical Review' English Linguistics Research. 3(1).

Amery, C (2009) 'Nikolaus Pevsner's 'Pioneers of the Modern Movement', 1936' The Burlington Magazine. 151(1278).

Anantharaman, M (2018) 'Critical sustainable consumption: a research agenda' Journal of Environmental Studies and Sciences. 8. pp 553–561.

Art Pills (2019) What Do We Mean by Fine Art? Kooness. March 7th. Available at: (Accessed on: 09/07/2022).

Arts Council England (2011) Arts audiences: insight.

Arts Council England (2020) Let's Create: Our Strategy 2020-2030.

Baldwin, J. Pingault, J. Schoeler, T. Sallis, H. Munafo, M (2022) 'Protecting against researcher bias in secondary data analysis: challenges and potential solutions' European Journal of Epidemiology. 37. Pp 1–10.

Bates, T (1975) 'Gramsci and the Theory of Hegemony' Journal of the History of Ideas. 36(2) pp, 351-366.

Beaudry, F (2021) How Does Nitrogen Oxide Pollution Affect the Environment? Treehugger. March 23rd. Available at: https://www.treehugger.com/what-is-nitrogen-oxide-pollution-1204135 (Accessed on: 20/07/2022).

Benjamin, W (1969) 'The Work of Art in the Age of Mechanical Reproduction' Illuminations. New York: Schocken Books.

Berg, B. L. (2007). Qualitative research methods for the social sciences. London: Pearson

Berndt, A.E (2020) 'Sampling Methods' Journal of Human Lactation. 36(2), pp 223-226.

Bhatt, C (2020) Sustainability and the Arts: Julie's Bicycle. Arts Help.

Braun V, Clarke V. 2006. Using thematic analysis in psychology. Qual Res Psychol. 3(2):77– 101.

Brown, N (2019) Autonomy: The Social Ontology of Art under Capitalism. Duke University Press:

Buckingham, F (2015) The art of effective protest: from flamenco flash mobs to craftivism. The Guardian. December 29th. Available at: https://www.theguardian.com/sustainable-business/2015/dec/29/art-effective-protest-campaigners-environmental-social-greenpeace-waste-banks-flash-mobs (Accessed on: 08/08/2022).

Burghardt, T. Pashkevich, A. Zakowska, L (2016) 'Influence of Volatile Organic Compounds Emissions from Road Marking Paints on Ground-level Ozone Formation: Case Study of Kraków, Poland'

Transportation Research Procedia. 14, pp. 714-723.

CCAC (2022) Tropospheric ozone. Climate and Clean Air Coalition. Available at: https://www.ccacoalition.org/en/slcps/troposphe ric-ozone#:~:text=In%20the%20stratosphere%2C%2 0ozone%20protects,major%20component% 20of%20urban%20smog. (Accessed on: 22/07/2022)

Cambridge Dictionary (2022) Meaning of Fine Art in English. Cambridge Dictionary. Available at: https://dictionary.cambridge.org/di ctionary/english/fine-art (Accessed on 09/07/2022).

Cascone, S (2019) Do You Come From a Wealthy Family? You're More Likely to Become an Artist Than Someone From a Poorer Background. Artnet. 29th April. Available at: https://news.artnet.com/art-world/wealthy-people-likely-become-artists-1529341 (Accessed on 25/09/2022).

Chatterjee, S (2020) 'Postindustrialism and the Long Arts and Crafts Movement: between Britain, India, and the United States of America' British Art Studies 15.

Caust, J (2007) 'The arts, governments and money: do the arts have any value if they don't make money'

Christensen, I (2018) Your Paints May Contain Toxic Chemicals. Here's How to Avoid Harming Yourself and the Environment. Artsy. August 10th. Available at: https://www.artsy.net/article/artsy-editorial-paints-toxic-chemicals-avoid-harming- environment (Accessed on: 21/07/2022).

Clarke, R (2017) What Do Marxists Have to say About Art? Culture Matters. October 14th Available at: https://www.culturematters.org.uk/index.php/cultu re/theory/item/2626- what-do-marxists-have-to-say- about-art (Accessed on 14/08/2022).

ClientEarth (2022) Greenwashing Files: Shell. Available at: https://www.clientearth.org/projects/the- greenwashing-files/shell/ (Accessed on 25/09/2022)

Cohen, L., Manion, L., & Morison, K. (2007). Research Methods in Education. (6th ed.). London: Routledge

Cohen, S (2020) Economic Growth and Environmental Sustainability. State of the Planet. 27th January. Available at: https://news.climate.columbia.edu/2020/01/27/eco nomic-growth- environmental-sustainability/ (Accessed on: 12/09/2022).

Crawford, A (1997) 'Ideas and Objects: The Arts and Crafts Movement in Britain' Design Issues 13(1), pp. 15-26.

Cypress, B (2017) 'Rigor or Reliability and Validity in Qualitative Research: Perspectives, Strategies, Reconceptualization, and Recommendations' Dimens Crit Care Nurs. 36(4): 253-263.

Demos, T.J., 1969. The politics of sustainability: art and ecology. Radical nature: art and architecture for a changing planet, 2009, pp.17-30

Eden Gallery (2021) What is Fine Art? Art Blog, Fine Art. Eden Gallery. July 11th. Available at: https://www.eden-gallery.com/news/fine-art- definition (Accessed on: 09/07/2022).

Eden Gallery (2022) What is Applied Art. Art Blog. Available at: https://www.eden- gallery.com/news/what-is-applied-art (Accessed on

11/07/2022).

Eliasson, O. Behmann, S. Garrison, G. Lutz, M. Thomas, M. Maurer, L. Kampe, B. Welte, R. Kraczon, K. Palermo, K. Wagner, K. Engberg-Pederson, A. Zanko, V. Eggel, C (2020) Fourteen views of Studio Olafur Eliasson's sustainability agenda. Olafur Eliasson: Sometimes the river is the bridge, 142-150. Available at: https://olafureliasson.net/archive/read/MDA12309 4/fourteen-views-of-studio-olafur- eliassons-sustainability-agenda#slideshow (Accessed on 29/09/2022).

Espinosa, A (2022) From Plastic Debris to Sculptures: Aurora Robson. Luxiders. N.d. Available at: https://luxiders.com/aurora-robson/ (Accessed on: 22/08/2022)

Fresia, J (2019) THREE WAYS CAPITALISM IMPACTS THE INSIDER ART WORLD.
KDOUTSIDEART. December 11th Available at: https://kdoutsiderart.com/2019/12/11/three- ways-capitalism-impacts-the-insider-art-world/ (Accessed on: 08/08/2022).

Galdas, P (2017) 'Revisiting Bias in Qualitative Research: Reflections on Its Relationship With Funding and Impact' International Journal of Qualitative Methods. 16.

Geiger, N. Swim, J. Fraser, J (2017) 'Catalyzing Public Engagement with Climate Change Through Informal Science Learning Centers' Science Communication. 39(2). Pp 221-249.

Graf, S (2022) An Introduction to the Arts and Crafts Movement. The Collector. February 14th. Available at: https://www.thecollector.com/introduction-arts-and-crafts-movement/ (Accessed on: 31/08/2022).

Gramsci, A (1971) Selections from The Prison Notebooks. ElecBook: London 1999.

General Kinematics (2020) The Metal Casting Process Explained. General Kinematics Blog. Available at: https://www.generalkinematics.com/blog/metal-casting-process-explained/ (Accessed on: 22/07/2022).

Gill, R. & Pratt, A.C. (2008) 'In the social factory? Immaterial labour precariousness and cultural work' Theory, Culture & Society, 25(7-8), pp. 1-30.

Gormley, A (2022) Sculpture Overview. Available at: https://www.antonygormley.com/works/sculpture/overview (Accessed on 12/09/2022)

Golbabaei, F & Khadem, M (2015) 'Air Pollution in Welding Processes — Assessment and
    Control Methods' Current Air Quality Issues.' IntechOpen: London.

Greene, J. Kisida, B. Bowen, D (2020) The Educational Value of Field Trips. Education Next. 14(1).

Greener Ideal (2021) The Impact of Metal Extraction on the Environment, Economy, and Society. The Greener Ideal Blog. March 10th. Available at: https://greenerideal.com/news/business/0617-metal-extraction/ (Accessed on: 22/07/2022).

Harris, G (2019) Antony Gormley criticises huge carbon footprint of the art world—but admits he is part of the problem. The Art Newspaper. September 10. Available at: https://www.theartnewspaper.com/2019/09/10/a

ntony-gormley-criticises-huge-carbon-footprint-of-the-art-worldbut-admits-he-is-part-of-the-problem (Accessed on: 01/08/2022).

Harris, G (2022) National Portrait Gallery in London ends BP sponsorship after 30 years. The Art Newspaper. February 22nd. Available at: https://www.theartnewspaper.com /2022/02/22/national-portrait-gallery-in-london-ends- bp-sponsorship-after-30-years (Accessed on: 15/08/2022).

Helmenstine, A (2020) Fractional Distillation Definition and Examples. ThoughtCo. February 19. Available at: https://www.thoughtco.com/definition-of-fractional-distillation-604421 (Accessed on: 27/02/2022).

Henderson-Sellers, A & Hughes, N.A (1982) 'Albedo and its importance in climate theory'
Progress in Physical Geography: Earth and Environment. 6(1). pp 1-44.

Howarth, D (2015) 'Gramsci, Hegemony and Post-Marxism' Antonio Gramsci. Critical Explorations in Contemporary Political Thought. Palgrave Macmillan, London.

Hu, J (2013) 'Evolving Paradigms of Manufacturing: From Mass Production to Mass Customization and Personalization' Procedia CIRP. 7. pp 3-8.

Hyde, K (2000) 'Recognising deductive processes in qualitative research' Qualitative Market Research. 3(2), 82-90.

Joshi, D. Modi, Y. Ravi, B (2011) 'EVALUATING ENVIRONMENTAL IMPACTS OF SAND CAST PRODUCTS USING LIFE CYCLE

ASSESSMENT' Conference Paper, Research into Design — Supporting Sustainable Product Development.

Julie's Bicycle (2022) About Us. Julie's Bicycle. Available at: https://juliesbicycle.com/about- us/ (Accessed on: 05/08/2022).

Julie's Bicycle (2018) Ice Watch London. Julie's Bicycle. November 8th. Available at: https://juliesbicycle.com/news-opinion/ice-watch-london-2018/(Accessed on: 05/08/2022).

Kagan, S (2014) 'The practice of ecological art' Plastik. 4.

Kang, D (2010) 'Understanding of consumption behaviors in art and cultural sectors for developing successful communication plans' Journal of Targeting, Measurement and Analysis for Marketing. 18. Pp 263-279.

Kaplan, W (2004) The Arts & Crafts Movement in Europe & America: Design for the Modern World. Thames & Hudson: Los Angeles.

Kettell, S (2006) 'Circuits of Capital and Overproduction: A Marxist Analysis of the Present World Economic Crisis' Review of Radical Political Economics. 38(1).

Krugh, M (2014) 'Joy in Labour: The Politicization of Craft from the Arts and Crafts Movement to Etsy' Canadian Review of American Studies. 44(2), pp. 281-301.

Kris, K (1997) 'Introduction: The Grand Tour' Eighteenth-Century Studies. 31(1).

Kumar, M (2022) Importance of Art to an Individual, Society, and Country? Madhans Art. March 6th. Available at: https://madhansart.com/importance-

of-
art/#:~:text=Art%20teaches%20people%20to%20b
e%20accepting%20of%20different%20cultures,-
When%20we%20realize&text=Art%20breaks%20all
%20cultural%20boundaries,a%20signific
ant%20impact%20on%20Society. (Accessed on:
02/08/2022).

Lal, R (2004) 'Soil Carbon Sequestration Impacts on Global
Climate Change and Food Security'
Science. 304(5677).

Lawton, R., Fujiwara, D., Bakhshi, H., Mourato, S., Arber,
M (2021) Guidance Note:
How to quantify the public benefit of your Art
Gallery using Value estimates. Arts Council
England.

Lebre, E. Stringer, M. Svobodova, K. Owen, J. Kemp, D.
Cote, C. Arratia-Solar, A. Valenta, R (2020) 'The social
and environmental complexities of extracting energy
transition metals' Nature Communications. 11, 4823.

Lescaze, Z (2022) How Should Art Reckon with Climate
Change? The New York Times. March 25. Available
at: https://www.nytimes.com/2022/03/25/t-
magazine/art-climate- change.html (Accessed on:
01/08/2022).

Leung, L (2015) 'Validity, reliability, and generalizability in
qualitative research' J Family Med Prim Care. 4(3):
324-327.

Long-Sutehall, T. Sque, M. Addington-Hall, J (2010)
'Secondary analysis of qualitative data: a valuable
method for exploring sensitive issues with an elusive
population?' Journal of Research in Nursing. 16(4)
335–344.

Luckeneder, S. Giljum, S. Schaffartzik, A. Maus, V. Tost, M (2021) 'Surge in global metal
mining threatens vulnerable ecosystems' Global Environmental Change. 69.

Lynch K & Kalaitzake, M (2018) 'Affective and calculative solidarity: The impact of
individualism and neoliberal capitalism' European Journal of Social Theory. 23(2).

Lyons, J (2017) 'Epistemological Problems of Perception' The Stanford Encyclopedia of Philosophy.

Lyon, T. P & Maxwell, J. W (2011). 'Greenwash: Corporate environmental disclosure under threat of audit' Journal of Economics & Management Strategy, 20, 3-41.

Machinery Future (2020) What is Metal Welding. Machinery Future. August 7th. Available at: https://machineryfuture.weebly.com/knowledge/what-is-metal-welding (Accessed on: 22/07/2022).

Martin, M (2019) The Science of Painting: Oil Paint and the Environment. Artful Scientist. May 28th. Available at: https://artfulscientist.home.blog/2019/05/28/the-science-of- painting-oil-paint-and-the-environment/ (Accessed on: 20/07/2022).

Marx, K 1818-1883. (1996). The Communist manifesto. London; Chicago, Ill.: Pluto Press.

Maynard, D.W. Schaeffer, N.C. Freese, J (2011). Improving Response Rates in Telephone Interviews. In: Antaki, C. (eds) Applied Conversation Analysis. Palgrave Advances in Linguistics. Palgrave Macmillan, London.

McMillan, K (2020) Could contemporary art be less wasteful? Apollo Magazine. January 27th. Available at: https://www.apollo-magazine.com/contemporary-art-waste-kate-mcmillan- niru-ratnam/ (Accessed on: 02/08/2022).

McPherson, J & Mazza, N (2014) 'Using Arts Activism and Poetry to Catalyze Human Rights Engagement and Reflection' Social Work Education. 33(7). Pp- 944-958.

Mumford, A (2016) Why BP has no place in our arts. OpenDemocracy. March 5th. Available at: https://www.opendemocracy.net/en/opendemocrac yuk/why-bp-has-no-place-in-our- arts/ (Accessed on: 12/09/2022)

Nelson, R (2014) The artworld and the paradox of sustainability. Sustainable? On artworld and real-world ecologies. Artlink. 34:4. December.

Neuendorf, K (2018) Content analysis and thematic analysis. In Advanced Research Methods for Applied Psychology. Routledge.

Ng, E. Chen, D. Edis, R (2016) Nitrogen pollution: the forgotten element of climate change. The Conversation. December 4th. Available at: https://theconversation.com/nitrogen- pollution-the-forgotten-element-of-climate-change-69348#:~:text=Nitrogenous%20gases%20also%20pl ay%20an,the%20atmosphere%20than%2 0carbon%20dioxide. (Accessed on: 22/07/2022),

Noble, H & Smith, J (2015) 'Issues of validity and reliability in qualitative research' Evidence- Based Nursing. 18: 34-35.

Oliver, S. (2004) 'Basil Oliver and the End of the Arts and Crafts Movement' Architectural History, 47, pp. 329-360.

Paiano, A. Pontrandolfo, A. Lagioia, G. Gallucci, T (2021) 'Sustainable options for paints through a life cycle assessment method' Journal of Cleaner Production. 295.

Pollution Issues (2008) How Paint Pollution Effects the Environment. Pollution Issues. November 19th. Available at: https://pollutionissues.co.uk/how-paint-pollution-effects- environment/ (Accessed on: 21/07/2022).

Pritchard, S (2018) Time to take art back from the capitalists: a brief history of art and artwashing. Culture Matters. February 15th. Available at: https://www.culturematters.org.uk/index.php/cultu re/theory/item/2736-time-to-take-art- back-from-the-capitalists-a-brief-history-of-art-and-artwashing (Accessed on: 14/08/2022).

Raworth, K (2017) 'A Doughnut for the Anthropocene: humanity's compass in the 21st century' The Lancet; Planetary Health. 1(2).

Rea, N (2019) What Would It Cost for the Art World to Offset Its Enormous Carbon Footprint? We've Compiled a Helpful Menu of Prices. Artnet. Available at: https://news.artnet.com/art-world/carbon-offset-art-world-1720782 (Accessed on: 01/08/2022)

Rise Art (2022) A Guide to the Feminist Art Movement's History & Contemporary Impact. Rise Art. Available at: https://www.riseart.com/guide/2418/guide-to-the-feminist-art-movement#:~:text=The%20Feminist%20Art%20m ovement%20emerged,gender%20stereoty pes%20in%20the%20arts.   (Accessed   on: 09/07/2022).

Rogers, J (2020) The Interpretivist Lens – What Design Study as a Method of Inquiry Can Teach Us. Visualization Design Lab. October 30th. Available at: https://vdl.sci.utah.edu/blog/2020/10/30/interpret-lens/#:~:text=Interpretivism%20stands%20in%20contrast%20to,based%20on%20their%20personal%20experience. (Accessed on: 14/09/2022).

Rowe, W (2014) Positionality. In D. Coghlan, & M. Brydon-Miller (Eds.), The SAGE encyclopedia of action research (pp. 628-628). SAGE Publications Ltd.

Rosengarten, F (1986) 'Gramsci's Arrest' Italian Culture. 7(1), p 71-80

Saunders, M.N.K., Lewis, P. & Thornhill, A., (2019) Research methods for business students Eighth.

Schwartz, J (2014) Soil as Carbon Storehouse: New Weapon in Climate Fight? Yale Environment 360. March 4th. Available   at: https://e360.yale.edu/features/soil_as_carbon_storehouse_new_weapon_in_climate_fight #:~:text=The%20degradation%20of%20soils%20from,CO2%20and%20slowing%20climate%2 0change. (Accessed on: 27/07/2022).

Sharma, G (2017) 'Pros and cons of different sampling techniques' International Journal of Applied Research. 3(7), pp- 749-752.

Shell (2022) THE ART OF COLLABORATION. Shell. Available   at: https://www.shell.com/inside-energy/the-art-of-collaboration.html# (Accessed on 26/09/2022)

Siegle, L (2012) Ethical living: can art be environmentally friendly? The Guardian. April 15th. Available at: https://www.theguardian.com/environment/2012/apr/15/lucy-siegle-ethical- art-paint (Accessed on: 02/08/2022).

Singh, S (2022) How the Arts and Crafts Movement Rebelled Against the Machine Age. Owlcation. 4th April. Available at: https://owlcation.com/humanities/How-The-Arts-and- Crafts-Movement-Reacted-Against-the-Machine-Age (Accessed on 11/01/2022).

Sinnett, D & Sardo, A (2020) 'Former metal mining landscapes in England and Wales: Five perspectives from local residents' Landscape and Urban Planning. 193.

Slotover, M (2021) The Art World Is Finally Talking About Offsetting Its Carbon Footprint. This Simple Approach Might Be the Most Effective Way to Do That. Artnet. January 29. Available at: https://news.artnet.com/sustainability/art-world-carbon-offsetting-options- 1940363 (Accessed on: 17/07/2022).

Sommer, L. Swim, J. Keller, A. Klockner, C (2019) '"Pollution Pods": The merging of art and psychology to engage the public in climate change' Global Environmental Change. 59.

Sommer, L & Klockner, C (2021) 'Does Activist Art Have the Capacity to Raise Awareness in Audiences? —A Study on Climate Change Art at the ArtCOP21 Event in Paris' Psychology of Aesthetics, Creativity, and the Arts. 15(1). 60-75.

Stanfield, S (2022) Are Oil Paints Eco-Friendly? 12

Important Questions Answered. Citizen Sustainable. June 18th. Available at: https://citizensustainable.com/oil-paints/#2_Are_Oil_Paints_Eco-Friendly (Accessed on: 21/07/2022).

Stanley, L. and S. Wise. (1993) Breaking Out Again: Feminist Ontology' and Epistemology'. London and New York: Routledge.

Stratton, S (2021) 'Population Research: Convenience Sampling Strategies' Prehospital and Disaster Medicine. 34(4).

Thornes, J (2008) A Rough Guide to Environmental Art. The Annual Review of Environment and Resources. July 29.

Throsby, D (1994) 'The Production and Consumption of the Arts: A View of Cultural
Economics' Journal of Economic Literature. 32(1). Pp 1-29.

Towner, J (1985) 'The Grand Tour: A Key Phase in the History of Tourism' Annals of Tourism Research. 12, pp. 297-333.

Tuckett, A (2004) 'Applying thematic analysis theory to practice: A researcher's experience'
Contemporary Nurse. 19(1-2), pp. 75-87.

Victoria and Albert Museum (2022) Arts and Crafts: an introduction. Victoria and Albert Musuem. Available at: https://www.vam.ac.uk/articles/arts-and-crafts-an- introduction#main-content (Accessed on 09/07/2022).

Wall, D. Najar, D. Hegel, G (2020) Art and Health: The Real-World Benefits of Viewing Art. Park West Gallery. April 15th. Available at:

https://www.parkwestgallery.com/art-and-health-the-benefits-of-viewing-art/ (Accessed on: 02/08/2022)

Watson, G (2018) The Process of Alkali Refining Linseed Oil. JUST PAINT. July 24th. Available at: https://justpaint.org/the-process-of-alkali-refining-linseed-oil/ (Accessed on: 21/07/2022).

Weber, E (2006) 'EXPERIENCE-BASED AND DESCRIPTION-BASED PERCEPTIONS OF LONG- TERM RISK: WHY GLOBAL WARMING DOES NOT SCARE US (YET)' Climate Change. 77. 130- 120.

Weidmann, T. Lenzen, M. Keyber, L. Steinberger, J (2020) 'Scientists' warning on affluence'
Nature Communications. 11.

Weisberger, M & Bradford, A (2021) Deductive reasoning vs. Inductive reasoning. Live Science. December 7th. Available at: https://www.livescience.com/21569-deduction-vs- induction.html (Accessed on: 06/09/2022)

Winter, R (1975) 'The Arts and Crafts as a Social Movement' Record of the Art Museum, Aspects of the Arts and Crafts Movement in America. 34(2). Pp 36-40.

Appendices

Victoria Slattery

Appendix One: Interview Questions

1. How concerned are you about the ongoing climate crisis on a scale of 1-10? 1 being not concerned and 10 being very concerned.

2. How sustainable do you believe the arts are on a scale of 1-10? 1 being not sustainable at all and 10 being extremely sustainable.

3. Do you try to include themes of environmental stewardship in your work?

And why is this?

4. Do you consider the environmental impacts of the mediums you utilise in your work?

And why is this?

5. Do you feel there is a social class divide within the arts and creative industries? And why?

7. Have you ever viewed a piece of art which has

motivated you to change your behaviour? And why? This does not necessarily have to relate to the climate crisis

8. Do you feel you need to continually be making work to stay relevant as an artist?

Appendix Two: Blank Consent Form

Informed Consent Form

An overview and collection of consent for participants taking part in semi-structured interviews regarding their artistic practice/ creative job role.

This study will require you to answer a sequence of questions delivered to you by an interviewer. These questions will concern your artists practice/job role and are designed for you to express your thoughts/ feelings, regarding the sustainability of the methods and materials used by you and your colleagues. The information you provide will be used in a study regarding the sustainability of Fine Art and its ability to influence positive cultural and political change.

I.................................voluntarily   agree   to participate in this research study.

I understand that even if I agree to participate now, I can withdraw at any time or refuse to answer any question without any consequences of any kind.

I understand that I can withdraw permission to use data from my interview within two weeks after the interview, in which case the material will be deleted.

I have had the purpose and nature of the study explained to me in writing and I have had the opportunity to ask questions about the study.

I understand that I will not benefit directly from participating in this research.

I agree to my interview being audio-recorded.

I understand that all information I provide for this study will be treated confidentially.

I understand that disguised extracts from my interview may be quoted in this dissertation.

I understand that signed co consent forms and original audio recordings will be retained until the exam board confirms the results of their dissertation.

I understand that under freedom of information legalisation I am entitled to access the information

I have provided at any time while it is in storage as specified above.

I understand that I am free to contact any of the people involved in the research to seek further clarification and information.

If you wish to contact the supervisor of this research, please see the contact details below

Richard Kotter
e-mail: richard.kotter@northumbria.ac.uk

Signature of research participant

Signature of participant
Date

Signature of researcher

I believe the participant is giving informed consent to participate in this study

Signature of researcher
Date

BOOM!

This book was originally submitted as a dissertation in partial fulfilment of the requirements of an MSc in Disaster Management and Sustainable Development at Northumbria University, Newcastle (UK).

Victoria Slattery

A note about Boom Graduates

We propel graduates forward so they can make their mark on the world - we push the boundaries, share brilliant ideas and inspire possibility. We publish dissertations as books, presented gift-boxed at graduation ceremonies, delivering brand-new research to the world quicker than anyone else. We plant trees for every commissioned book sold, and give our Boom graduates the chance to profit-share from their brilliant ideas. Furthermore we donate the majority of our profits to funding research and scholarship for disadvantaged students who wouldn't normally be able to attend university. Through academic excellence and environmental sustainability, *Boom Graduates* are changing the world.

We are Boom Graduates - an imprint of Boom Publications Ltd. We are a more-than-profit company, dedicating over half our profits to providing university scholarships for underprivileged students across the world. We aim to become the globe's biggest provider of such scholarships – and if like Victoria, the author of this book, you'd also like to contribute to making the world a better place, please contact us: we publish monographs, edited books, and moreover our graduate series – Boom Graduates – are presented at graduation days across the world in archival, lined museum-quality presentation cases, engraved with the graduate's name and award.

Boom Publications are based at the Duncan of Jordanstone College of Art and Design, at the University of Dundee in Scotland. We were one of the winners of the 2022 Venture awards hosted by the Centre for Entrepreneurship, and have since been shortlisted for the Converge Challenge, a national award that brings together ambitious and creative thinkers with innovative ideas to work with industry experts to transform their ideas into sustainable companies operating in the commercial world. We are also climate conscious and work with agencies to plant a tree for each and every book commissioned, offsetting thousands of tonnes of carbon each year. Follow us on social media to watch our forest grow @boomgraduates.

Thank you for contributing by purchasing this book. Please visit our catalogues on www.boompublications.com.

Victoria Slattery

Notes

Victoria Slattery